FOR THE TIME BEING

FOR
THE TIME BEING

BY

W. H. AUDEN

FABER AND FABER

*First published in mcmxlv
by Faber and Faber Limited
24 Russell Square London W.C.1.
Second impression mcmliii
Third impression mcmlviii
Printed in Great Britain by
Bradford and Dickens
Drayton House London W.C.1.*

CONTENTS

THE SEA AND THE MIRROR

A Commentary on Shakespeare's
The Tempest

TO JAMES AND TANIA STERN

And am I wrong to worship where
Faith cannot doubt nor Hope despair
Since my own soul can grant my prayer?
Speak, God of Visions, plead for me
And tell why I have chosen thee.

                              EMILY BRONTË

PREFACE

(The Stage Manager to the Critics)

The aged catch their breath,
For the nonchalant couple go
Waltzing across the tightrope
As if there were no death
Or hope of falling down;
The wounded cry as the clown
Doubles his meaning, and O
How the dear little children laugh
When the drums roll and the lovely
Lady is sawn in half.

O what authority gives
Existence its surprise?
Science is happy to answer
That the ghosts who haunt our lives
Are handy with mirrors and wire,
That song and sugar and fire,
Courage and come-hither eyes

Have a genius for taking pains.
But how does one think up a habit?
Our wonder, our terror remains.

Art opens the fishiest eye
To the Flesh and the Devil who heat
The Chamber of Temptation
Where heroes roar and die.
We are wet with sympathy now;
Thanks for the evening; but how
Shall we satisfy when we meet,
Between Shall-I and I-Will,
The lion's mouth whose hunger
No metaphors can fill?

Well, who in his own backyard
Has not opened his heart to the smiling
Secret he cannot quote?
Which goes to show that the Bard
Was sober when he wrote
That this world of fact we love
Is unsubstantial stuff:
All the rest is silence
On the other side of the wall;
And the silence ripeness,
And the ripeness all.

Chapter I

PROSPERO TO ARIEL

Stay with me, Ariel, while I pack, and with your first free
   act
   Delight my leaving; share my resigning thoughts
As you have served my revelling wishes: then, brave spirit,
   Ages to you of song and daring, and to me
Briefly Milan, then earth. In all, things have turned out
      better
   Than I once expected or ever deserved;
I am glad that I did not recover my dukedom till
   I do not want it; I am glad that Miranda
No longer pays me any attention; I am glad I have freed
      you,
   So at last I can really believe I shall die.
For under your influence death is inconceivable:
   On walks through winter woods, a bird's dry carcass
Agitates the retina with novel images,
   A stranger's quiet collapse in a noisy street
Is the beginning of much lively speculation,
   And every time some dear flesh disappears
What is real is the arriving grief; thanks to your service,
   The lonely and unhappy are very much alive.

But now all these heavy books are no use to me any more,
      for
   Where I go, words carry no weight: it is best,
Then, I surrender their fascinating counsel
   To the silent dissolution of the sea
Which misuses nothing because it values nothing;
   Whereas man overvalues everything
Yet, when he learns the price is pegged to his valuation,

9

Complains bitterly he is being ruined which, of course, he
    is,
So kings find it odd they should have a million subjects
    Yet share in the thoughts of none, and seducers
Are sincerely puzzled at being unable to love
    What they are able to possess; so, long ago,
In an open boat, I wept at giving a city,
    Common warmth and touching substance, for a gift
In dealing with shadows. If age, which is certainly
    Just as wicked as youth, look any wiser,
It is only that youth is still able to believe
    It will get away with anything, while age
Knows only too well that it has got away with nothing:
    The child runs out to play in the garden, convinced
That the furniture will go on with its thinking lesson,
    Who, fifty years later, if he plays at all,
Will first ask its kind permission to be excused.

When I woke into my life, a sobbing dwarf
Whom giants served only as they pleased, I was not what
    I seemed;
    Beyond their busy backs I made a magic
To ride away from a father's imperfect justice,
    Take vengeance on the Romans for their grammar,
Usurp the popular earth and blot out for ever
    The gross insult of being a mere one among many:
Now, Ariel, I am that I am, your late and lonely master,
    Who knows now what magic is;—the power to enchant
That comes from disillusion. What the books can teach one
    Is that most desires end up in stinking ponds,
But we have only to learn to sit still and give no orders,
    To make you offer us your echo and your mirror;
We have only to believe you, then you dare not lie;
    To ask for nothing, and at once from your calm eyes,
With their lucid proof of apprehension and disorder,
    All we are not stares back at what we are. For all things
10

In your company, can be themselves: historic deeds
  Drop their hauteur and speak of shabby childhoods
When all they longed for was to join in the gang of doubts
  Who so tormented them; sullen diseases
Forget their dreadful appearance and make silly jokes;
  Thick-headed goodness for once is not a bore.
No one but you had sufficient audacity and eyesight
  To find those clearings where the shy humiliations
Gambol on sunny afternoons, the waterhole to which
  The scarred rogue sorrow comes quietly in the small
      hours:
And no one but you is reliably informative on hell;
  As you whistle and skip past, the poisonous
Resentments scuttle over your unrevolted feet,
  And even the uncontrollable vertigo,
Because it can scent no shame, is unobliged to strike.

> *Could he but once see Nature as*
>   *In truth she is for ever,*
> *What oncer would not fall in love?*
> *Hold up your mirror, boy, to do*
>   *Your vulgar friends this favour:*
> *One peep, though, will be quite enough;*
>   *To those who are not true,*
> *A statue with no figleaf has*
>   *A pornographic flavour.*

> *Inform my hot heart straight away*
>   *Its treasure loves another*
> *But turn to neutral topics then,*
> *Such as the pictures in this room,*
>   *Religion or the Weather;*
> *Pure scholarship in Where and When,*
>   *How Often and With Whom,*
> *Is not for Passion that must play*
>   *The Jolly Elder Brother.*

11

Be frank about our heathen foe,
For Rome will be a goner
If you soft-pedal the loud beast;
Describe in plain four-letter words
This dragon that's upon her:
But should our beggars ask the cost,
Just whistle like the birds;
Dare even Pope or Caesar know
The price of faith and honour?

Today I am free and no longer need your freedom:
You, I suppose, will be off now to look for likely victims;
　Crowds chasing ankles, lone men stalking glory,
Some feverish young rebel among amiable flowers
　In consultation with his handsome envy,
A punctual plump judge, a fly-weight hermit in a dream
　Of gardens that time is for ever outside—
To lead absurdly by their self-important noses.
　Are you malicious by nature? I don't know.
Perhaps only incapable of doing nothing or of
　Being by yourself, and, for all your wry faces
May secretly be anxious and miserable without
　A master to need you for the work you need.
Are all your tricks a test? If so, I hope you find, next time,
　Someone in whom you cannot spot the weakness
Through which you will corrupt him with your charm.
　　　Mine you did.
And me you have: thanks to us both, I have broken
Both of the promises I made as an apprentice;—
　To hate nothing and to ask nothing for its love.
All by myself I tempted Antonio into treason;
　However that could be cleared up; both of us know
That both were in the wrong, and neither need be sorry:
　But Caliban remains my impervious disgrace.
We did it, Ariel, between us; you found on me a wish
　For absolute devotion; result—his wreck

That sprawls in the weeds and will not be repaired:
   My dignity discouraged by a pupil's curse,
I shall go knowing and incompetent into my grave.

   The extravagant children, who lately swaggered
Out of the sea like gods, have, I think, been soundly hunted
   By their own devils into their human selves:
To all, then, but me, their pardons. Alonso's heaviness
   Is lost; and weak Sebastian will be patient
In future with his slothful conscience—after all, it pays;
   Stephano is contracted to his belly, a minor
But a prosperous kingdom; stale Trinculo receives,
   Gratis, a whole fresh repertoire of stories, and
Our younger generation its independent joy.
   Their eyes are big and blue with love; its lighting
Makes even us look new: yes, today it all looks so easy.
   Will Ferdinand be as fond of a Miranda
Familiar as a stocking? Will a Miranda who is
   No longer a silly lovesick little goose,
When Ferdinand and his brave world are her profession,
   Go into raptures over existing at all?
Probably I over-estimate their difficulties;
   Just the same, I am very glad I shall never
Be twenty and have to go through that business again,
   The hours of fuss and fury, the conceit, the expense.

> Sing first that green remote Cockagne
>   Where whiskey-rivers run,
> And every gorgeous number may
>   Be laid by anyone;
> For medicine and rhetoric
>   Lie mouldering on shelves,
> While sad young dogs and stomach-aches
>   Love no one but themselves.

13

Tell then of witty angels who
Come only to the beasts,
Of Heirs Apparent who prefer
Low dives to formal feasts;
For shameless Insecurity
Prays for a boot to lick,
And many a sore bottom finds
A sorer one to kick.

Wind up, though, on a moral note;—
That Glory will go bang,
Schoolchildren shall co-operate,
And honest rogues must hang;
Because our sound committee man
Has murder in his heart:
But should you catch a living eye,
Just wink as you depart.

Now our partnership is dissolved, I feel so peculiar:
    As if I had been on a drunk since I was born
And suddenly now, and for the first time, am cold sober,
    With all my unanswered wishes and unwashed days
Stacked up all round my life; as if through the ages I had
        dreamed
    About some tremendous journey I was taking,
Sketching imaginary landscapes, chasms and cities,
    Cold walls, hot spaces, wild mouths, defeated backs,
Jotting down fictional notes on secrets overheard
    In theatres and privies, banks and mountain inns,
And now, in my old age, I wake, and this journey really
        exists,
    And I have actually to take it, inch by inch,
Alone and on foot, without a cent in my pocket,
    Through a universe where time is not foreshortened,
No animals talk, and there is neither floating nor playing.

14

When I am safely home, oceans away in Milan, and
Realize once and for all I shall never see you again,
    Over there, maybe, it won't seem quite so dreadful
Not to be interesting any more, but an old man
    Just like other old men, with eyes that water
Easily in the wind, and a head that nods in the sunshine,
    Forgetful, maladroit, a little grubby,
And to like it. When the servants settle me into a chair
    In some well-sheltered corner of the garden,
And arrange my muffler and rugs, shall I ever be able
    To stop myself from telling them what I am doing,—
Sailing alone, out over seventy thousand fathoms—?
    Yet if I speak, I shall sink without a sound
Into unmeaning abysses. Can I learn to suffer
    Without saying something ironic or funny
On suffering? I never suspected the way of truth
    Was a way of silence where affectionate chat
Is but a robbers' ambush and even good music
    In shocking taste; and you, of course, never told me.
If I peg away at it honestly every moment,
    And have luck, perhaps by the time death pounces
His stumping question, I shall just be getting to know
    The difference between moonshine and daylight. . . .
I see you starting to fidget. I forgot. To you
    That doesn't matter. My dear, here comes Gonzalo
With a solemn face to fetch me. O Ariel, Ariel,
    How I shall miss you. Enjoy your element. Good-bye.

        Sing, Ariel, sing,
        Sweetly, dangerously
        Out of the sour
        And shiftless water,
        Lucidly out
        Of the dozing tree,
        Entrancing, rebuking
        The raging heart
        15

With a smoother song
Than this rough world,
Unfeeling god.

O brilliantly, lightly,
Of separation,
Of bodies and death,
Unanxious one, sing
To man, meaning me,
As now, meaning always,
In love or out,
Whatever that mean,
Trembling he takes
The silent passage
Into discomfort.

Chapter II

THE SUPPORTING CAST
SOTTO VOCE

ANTONIO

As all the pigs have turned back into men
And the sky is auspicious and the sea
Calm as a clock, we can all go home again.

Yes, it undoubtedly looks as if we
Could take life as easily now as tales
Write ever-after: not only are the

Two heads silhouetted against the sails
—And kissing, of course—well-built, but the lean
Fool is quite a person, the fingernails

Of the dear old butler for once quite clean,
And the royal passengers quite as good
As rustics, perhaps better, for they mean

What they say, without, as a rustic would,
Casting reflections on the courtly crew.
Yes, Brother Prospero, your grouping could

Not be more effective: given a few
Incomplete objects and a nice warm day,
What a lot a little music can do.

Dotted about the deck they doze or play,
Your loyal subjects all, grateful enough
To know their place and believe what you say.

Antonio, sweet brother, has to laugh.
How easy you have made it to refuse
Peace to your greatness! Break your wand in half,

The fragments will join; burn your books or lose
Them in the sea, they will soon reappear,
Not even damaged: as long as I choose

To wear my fashion, whatever you wear
Is a magic robe; while I stand outside
Your circle, the will to charm is still there.

As I exist so you shall be denied,
Forced to remain our melancholy mentor,
The grown-up man, the adult in his pride,

Never have time to curl up at the centre
Time turns on when completely reconciled,
Never become and therefore never enter
The green occluded pasture as a child.

> *Your all is partial, Prospero;*
> *My will is all my own:*
> *Your need to love shall never know*
> *Me: I am I, Antonio,*
> *By choice myself alone.*

FERDINAND

Flesh, fair, unique, and you, warm secret that my kiss
Follows into meaning Miranda, solitude
Where my omissions are, still possible, still good,
Dear Other at all times, retained as I do this,

From moment to moment as you enrich them so
Inherit me, my cause, as I would cause you now

With mine your sudden joy, two wonders as one vow
Pre-empting all, here, there, for ever, long ago.

I would smile at no other promise than touch, taste,
      sight,
Were there not, my enough, my exaltation, to bless
As world is offered world, as I hear it tonight

Pleading with ours for us, another tenderness
That neither without either could or would possess,
The Right Required Time, The Real Right Place, O Light.

> *One bed is empty, Prospero,*
>   *My person is my own;*
> *Hot Ferdinand will never know*
> *The flame with which Antonio*
>   *Burns in the dark alone.*

STEPHANO

Embrace me, belly, like a bride;
Dear daughter, for the weight you drew
From humble pie and swallowed pride,
Believe the boast in which you grew:
Where mind meets matter, both should woo;
Together let us learn that game
The high play better than the blue:
A lost thing looks for a lost name.

Behind your skirts your son must hide
When disappointments bark and boo;
Brush my heroic ghosts aside,
Wise nanny, with a vulgar pooh:
Exchanging cravings we pursue
Alternately a single aim:

19

Between the bottle and the 'loo'
A lost thing looks for a lost name.

Though in the long run satisfied,
The will of one by being two
At every moment is denied;
Exhausted glasses wonder who
Is self and sovereign, I or You?
We cannot both be what we claim,
The real Stephano—Which is true?
A lost thing looks for a lost name.

Child? Mother? Either grief will do;
The need for pardon is the same,
The contradiction is not new:
A lost thing looks for a lost name.

> *One glass is untouched, Prospero,*
> *My nature is my own;*
> *Inert Stephano does not know*
> *The feast at which Antonio*
> *Toasts One and One alone.*

GONZALO

Evening, grave, immense, and clear,
Overlooks our ship whose wake
Lingers undistorted on
Sea and silence; I look back
For the last time as the sun
Sets behind that island where
All our loves were altered: yes,
My prediction came to pass,
Yet I am not justified,
And I weep but not with pride.
Not in me the credit for

Words I uttered long ago
Whose glad meaning I betrayed;
Truths today admitted, owe
Nothing to the councillor
In whose booming eloquence
Honesty became untrue.
Am I not Gonzalo who
By his self-reflection made
Consolation an offence?

There was nothing to explain:
Had I trusted the Absurd
And straightforward note by note
Sung exactly what I heard,
Such immediate delight
Would have taken there and then
Our common welkin by surprise,
All would have begun to dance
Jigs of self-deliverance.
It was I prevented this,
Jealous of my native ear,
Mine the art which made the song
Sound ridiculous and wrong,
I whose interference broke
The gallop into jog-trot prose
And by speculation froze
Vision into an idea,
Irony into a joke,
Till I stood convicted of
Doubt and insufficient love.

Farewell, dear island of our wreck.
All have been restored to health,
All have seen the Commonwealth,
There is nothing to forgive.
Since a storm's decision gave

His subjective passion back
To a meditative man,
Even reminiscence can
Comfort ambient troubles like
Some ruined tower by the sea
Whence boyhoods growing and afraid
Learn a formula they need
In solving their mortality,
Even rusting flesh can be
A simple locus now, a bell
The Already There can lay
Hands on if at any time
It should feel inclined to say
To the lonely—'Here I am,'
To the anxious—'All is well.'

One tongue is silent, Prospero,
My language is my own;
Decayed Gonzalo does not know
The shadow that Antonio
Talks to, at noon, alone.

ADRIAN AND FRANCISCO

Good little sunbeams must learn to fly,
But it's madly ungay when the goldfish die.

One act is censored, Prospero,
My audience is my own;
Nor Adrian nor Francisco know
The drama that Antonio
Plays in his head alone.

ALONSO

Dear Son, when the warm multitudes cry,
Ascend your throne majestically,

But keep in mind the waters where fish
See sceptres descending with no wish
To touch them; sit regal and erect,
But imagine the sands where a crown
Has the status of a broken-down
Sofa or mutilated statue:
Remember as bells and cannon boom
The cold deep that does not envy you,
The sunburnt superficial kingdom
Where a king is an object.

Expect no help from others, for who
Talk sense to princes or refer to
The scorpion in official speeches
As they unveil some granite Progress
Leading a child and holding a bunch
Of lilies? In their Royal Zoos the
Shark and the octopus are tactfully
Omitted; synchronized clocks march on
Within their powers: without, remain
The ocean flats where no subscription
Concerts are given, the desert plain
Where there is nothing for lunch.

Only your darkness can tell you what
A prince's ornate mirror dare not,
Which you should fear more—the sea in which
A tyrant sinks entangled in rich
Robes while a mistress turns a white back
Upon his splutter, or the desert
Where an emperor stands in his shirt
While his diary is read by sneering
Beggars, and far off he notices
A lean horror flapping and hopping
Toward him with inhuman swiftness:
Learn from your dreams what you lack,

For as your fears are, so must you hope.
The Way of Justice is a tightrope
Where no prince is safe for one instant
Unless he trust his embarrassment,
As in his left ear the siren sings
Meltingly of water and a night
Where all flesh had peace, and on his right
The efreet offers a brilliant void
Where his mind could be perfectly clear
And all his limitations destroyed:
Many young princes soon disappear
To join all the unjust kings.

So, if you prosper, suspect those bright
Mornings when you whistle with a light
Heart. You are loved; you have never seen
The harbour so still, the park so green,
So many well-fed pigeons upon
Cupolas and triumphal arches,
So many stags and slender ladies
Beside the canals. Remember when
Your climate seems a permanent home
For marvellous creatures and great men,
What griefs and convulsions startled Rome,
Ecbatana, Babylon.

How narrow the space, how slight the chance
For civil pattern and importance
Between the watery vagueness and
The triviality of the sand,
How soon the lively trip is over
From loose craving to sharp aversion,
Aimless jelly to paralyzed bone:
At the end of each successful day
Remember that the fire and the ice
Are never more than one step away

24

From the temperate city; it is
But a moment to either.

But should you fail to keep your kingdom
And, like your father before you, come
Where thought accuses and feeling mocks,
Believe your pain: praise the scorching rocks
For their desiccation of your lust,
Thank the bitter treatment of the tide
For its dissolution of your pride,
That the whirlwind may arrange your will
And the deluge release it to find
The spring in the desert, the fruitful
Island in the sea, where flesh and mind
Are delivered from mistrust.

Blue the sky beyond her humming sail
As I sit today by our ship's rail
Watching exuberant porpoises
Escort us homeward and writing this
For you to open when I am gone:
Read it, Ferdinand, with the blessing
Of Alonso, your father, once King
Of Naples, now ready to welcome
Death, but rejoicing in a new love,
A new peace, having heard the solemn
Music strike and seen the statue move
To forgive our illusion.

> One crown is lacking, Prospero,
>   My empire is my own;
> Dying Alonso does not know
> The diadem Antonio
>   Wears in his world alone.

25

At Dirty Dick's and Sloppy Joe's
   We drank our liquor straight,
Some went upstairs with Margery,
   And some, alas, with Kate;
And two by two like cat and mouse
The homeless played at keeping house.

There Wealthy Meg, the Sailor's Friend,
   And Marion, cow-eyed,
Opened their arms to me but I
   Refused to step inside;
I was not looking for a cage
In which to mope in my old age.

The nightingales are sobbing in
   The orchards of our mothers,
And hearts that we broke long ago
   Have long been breaking others;
Tears are round, the sea is deep:
Roll them overboard and sleep.

One gaze points elsewhere, Prospero,
   My compass is my own;
Nostalgic sailors do not know
   The waters where Antonio
Sails on and on alone.

SEBASTIAN

My rioters all disappear, my dream
Where Prudence flirted with a naked sword,
Securely vicious, crumbles; it is day;
Nothing has happened; we are all alive:
I am Sebastian, wicked still, my proof
Of mercy that I wake without a crown.

What sadness signalled to our children's day
Where each believed all wishes wear a crown
And anything pretended is alive,
That one by one we plunged into that dream
Of solitude and silence where no sword
Will ever play once it is called a proof?

The arrant jewel singing in his crown
Persuaded me my brother was a dream
I should not love because I had no proof,
Yet all my honesty assumed a sword;
To think his death I thought myself alive
And stalked infected through the blooming day.

The lie of Nothing is to promise proof
To any shadow that there is no day
Which cannot be extinguished with some sword,
To want and weakness that the ancient crown
Envies the childish head, murder a dream
Wrong only while its victim is alive.

O blessed be bleak Exposure on whose sword,
Caught unawares, we prick ourselves alive!
Shake Failure's bruising fist! Who else would crown
Abominable error with a proof?
I smile because I tremble, glad today
To be ashamed, not anxious, not a dream.

Children are playing, brothers are alive,
And not a heart or stomach asks for proof
That all this dearness is no lovers' dream;
Just Now is what it might be every day,
Right Here is absolute and needs no crown,
Ermine or trumpets, protocol or sword.

27

In dream all sins are easy, but by day
It is defeat gives proof we are alive:
The sword we suffer is the guarded crown.

One face cries nothing, Prospero,
My conscience is my own;
Pallid Sebastian does not know
The dream in which Antonio
Fights the white bull alone.

TRINCULO

Mechanic, merchant, king,
Are warmed by the cold clown
Whose head is in the clouds
And never can get down.

Into a solitude
Undreamed of by their fat
Quick dreams have lifted me;
The north wind steals my hat.

On clear days I can see
Green acres far below,
And the red roof where I
Was Little Trinculo.

There lies that solid world
These hands can never reach;
My history, my love,
Is but a choice of speech.

A terror shakes my tree,
A flock of words fly out,
Whereat a laughter shakes
The busy and devout.

Wild images, come down
Out of your freezing sky,
That I, like shorter men,
May get my joke and die.

Our note is jarring, Prospero,
My humour is my own;
Tense Trinculo will never know
The paradox Antonio
Laughs at, in woods, alone.

MIRANDA

My Dear One is mine as mirrors are lonely,
As the poor and sad are real to the good king,
And the high green hill sits always by the sea.

Up jumped the Black Man behind the elder tree,
Turned a somersault and ran away waving;
My Dear One is mine as mirrors are lonely.

The Witch gave a squawk; her venomous body
Melted into light as water leaves a spring
And the high green hill sits always by the sea.

At his crossroads, too, the Ancient prayed for me;
Down his wasted cheeks tears of joy were running:
My Dear One is mine as mirrors are lonely.

He kissed me awake, and no one was sorry;
The sun shone on sails, eyes, pebbles, anything,
And the high green hill sits always by the sea.

So, to remember our changing garden, we
Are linked as children in a circle dancing:
My Dear One is mine as mirrors are lonely,
And the high green hill sits always by the sea.

29

One link is missing, Prospero,
    My magic is my own;
Happy Miranda does not know
The figure that Antonio,
The Only One, Creation's O
    Dances for Death alone.

Chapter III

CALIBAN TO THE AUDIENCE

If now, having dismissed your hired impersonators with verdicts tanging from the laudatory orchid to the disgusted and disgusting egg, you ask and, of course, notwithstanding the conscious fact of his irrevocable absence, you instinctively *do* ask for our so good, so great, so dead author to stand before the finally lowered curtain and take his shyly responsible bow for this, his latest, ripest production, it is I—my reluctance is, I can assure you, co-equal with your dismay—who will always loom thus wretchedly into your confused picture, for, in default of the all-wise, all explaining master you would speak *to*, who else at least can, who else indeed must respond to your bewildered cry, but its very echo, the begged question you would speak to him *about*.

★   ★   ★

We must own [*for the present I speak your echo*] to a nervous perplexity not unmixed, frankly, with downright resentment. How *can* we grant the indulgence for which in his epilogue your personified type of the creative so lamely, tamely pleaded? Imprisoned, by you, in the mood doubtful, loaded, by you, with distressing embarrassments, we are, we submit, in no position to set *anyone* free.

Our native Muse, heaven knows and heaven be praised, is not exclusive. Whether out of the innocence of a child-like heart to whom all things are pure, or with the serenity of a status so majestic that the mere keeping up of tones and appearances, the suburban wonder as to what the strait-laced Unities might possibly think, or sad sour Probability possibly say, are questions for which she doesn't because she needn't, she hasn't in her lofty maturity any

31

longer to care a rap, she invites, dear generous-hearted creature that she is, just *tout le monde* to drop in at any time so that her famous, memorable, sought-after evenings present to the speculative eye an ever-shining, never-tarnished proof of her amazing unheard-of power to combine and happily contrast, to make *every* shade of the social and moral palette contribute to the general richness, of the skill, unapproached and unattempted by Grecian aunt or Gaelic sister, with which she can skate full tilt toward the forbidden incoherence and then, in the last split second, on the shuddering edge of the bohemian standardless abyss effect her breathtaking triumphant turn.

No timid segregation by rank or taste for her, no prudent listing into those who will, who might, who certainly would not get on, no nicely graded scale of invitations to heroic formal Tuesdays, young comic Thursdays, al fresco farcical Saturdays. No, the real, the only test of the theatrical as of the gastronomic, her practice confidently wagers, is the mixed perfected brew.

As he looks in on her, so marvellously at home with all her cosy swarm about her, what accents will not assault the new arrival's ear, the magnificent tropes of tragic defiance and despair, the repartee of the high humour, the pun of the very low, cultured drawl and manly illiterate bellow, yet all of them gratefully doing their huge or tiny best to make the party go?

And if, assured by her smiling wave that of course he may, he should presently set out to explore her vast and rambling mansion, to do honour to its dear odd geniuses of local convenience and proportion, its multiplied deities of mysterious stair and interesting alcove, not one of the laughing groups and engrossed warmed couples that he keeps 'surprising'—the never-ending surprise for him is that he doesn't seem to—but affords some sharper instance of relations he would have been the last to guess at, choleric prince at his ease with lymphatic butler, moist

32

hand-taking so to dry, youth getting on quite famously with stingy cold old age, some stranger vision of the large loud liberty violently rocking yet never, he is persuaded, finally upsetting the jolly crowded boat.

What, he may well ask, has the gracious goddess done to all these people that, at her most casual hint, they should so trustingly, so immediately take off those heavy habits one thinks of them as having for their health and happiness day and night to wear, without in this unfamiliar un-buttoned state—the notable absence of the slightest shiver or not-quite-inhibited sneeze is indication positive—for a second feeling the draught? Is there, could there be, *any* miraculous suspension of the wearily historic, the dingily geographic, the dully drearily sensible beyond her faith, her charm, her love, to command? Yes, there could be, yes, alas, indeed yes, O there is, right here, right now before us, the situation present.

How *could* you, you who are one of the oldest habitués at these delightful functions, one, possibly the closest, of her trusted inner circle, how could you be guilty of the in-credible unpardonable treachery of bringing along the one creature, as you above all men must have known, whom she cannot and will not under any circumstances stand, the solitary exception she is not at any hour of the day or night at home to, the unique case that her attendant spirits have absolute instructions never, neither at the front door nor at the back, to admit?

At Him and at Him only does she draw the line, not be-cause there are any limits to her sympathy but precisely because there are none. Just because of all she is and all she means to be, she cannot conceivably tolerate in her presence the represented principle of *not* sympathizing, *not* associating, *not* amusing, the only child of her Awful Enemy, the rival whose real name she will never sully her lips with—'that envious witch' is sign sufficient—who does not rule but defiantly is the unrectored chaos.

c   33

All along and only too well she has known what would happen if, by any careless mischance—of conscious malice she never dreamed till now—He should ever manage to get in. She foresaw what He would do to the conversation, lying in wait for its vision of private love or public justice to warm to an Egyptian brilliance and then with some fish-like odour or *bruit insolite* snatching the visionaries back tongue-tied and blushing to the here and now; she foresaw what He would do to the arrangements, breaking, by a refusal to keep in step, the excellent order of the dancing ring, and ruining supper by knocking over the loaded appetizing tray; worst of all, she foresaw, she dreaded what He would end up by doing to her, that, not content with upsetting her guests, with spoiling their fun, His progress from outrage to outrage would not relent before the gross climax cf His making, horror unspeakable, a pass at her virgin self.

Let us suppose, even, that in your eyes she is by no means as we have always fondly imagined, your dear friend, that what we have just witnessed was not what it seemed to us, the inexplicable betrayal of a life-long sacred loyalty, but your long-premeditated just revenge, the final evening up of some ancient never-forgotten score, then even so, why make us suffer who have never, in all conscience, done you harm? Surely the theatrical relation, no less than the marital, is governed by the sanely decent general law that, before visitors, in front of the children or the servants, there shall be no indiscreet revelation of animosity, no 'scenes', that, no matter to what intolerable degrees of internal temperature and pressure restraint may raise both the injured and the guilty, nevertheless such restraint is applied to tones·and topics, the exhibited picture must be still as always the calm and smiling one the most malicious observer can see nothing wrong with, and not until the last of those whom manifested anger or mistrust would embarrass or amuse or not be good for have gone away or out or up, is the voice raised, the table

34

thumped, the suspicious letter snatched at or the outrageous bill furiously waved.

For we, after all—you cannot have forgotten this—are strangers to her. We have never claimed her acquaintance, knowing as well as she that we do not and never could belong on her side of the curtain. All we have ever asked for is that for a few hours the curtain should be left undrawn, so as to allow our humble ragged selves the privilege of craning and gaping at the splendid goings-on inside. We most emphatically do *not* ask that she should speak to us, or try to understand us; on the contrary our one desire has always been that she should preserve for ever her old high strangeness, for what delights us about her world is just that it neither is nor possibly could become one in which we could breathe or behave, that in her house the right of innocent passage should remain so universal that the same neutral space accommodates the conspirator and his victim; the generals of both armies, the chorus of patriots and the choir of nuns, palace and farmyard, cathedral and smugglers' cave, that time should never revert to that intransigent element we are so ineluctably and only too familiarly in, but remain the passive good-natured creature she and her friends can by common consent do anything they like with—(it is not surprising that they should take advantage of their strange power and so frequently skip hours and days and even years: the dramatic mystery is that they should always so unanimously agree upon exactly how many hours and days and years to skip)— that upon their special constitutions the moral law should continue to operate so exactly that the timid not only deserve but actually win the fair, and it is the socially and physically unemphatic David who lays low the gorilla-chested Goliath with one well-aimed custard pie, that in their blessed climate, the manifestation of the inner life should always remain so easy and habitual that a sudden eruption of musical and metaphorical power is instantly

35

recognized as standing for grief and disgust, an elegant *contrapposto* for violent death, and that consequently the picture which they in there present to us out here is always that of the perfectly tidiable case of disorder, the beautiful and serious problem exquisitely set without a single superfluous datum and insoluble with less, the expert landing of all the passengers with all their luggage safe and sound in the best of health and spirits and without so much as a scratch or a bruise.

Into that world of freedom without anxiety, sincerity without loss of vigour, feeling that loosens rather than ties the tongue, we are not, we reiterate, so blinded by presumption to our proper status and interest as to expect or even wish at any time to enter, far less to dwell there.

Must we—it seems oddly that we must—remind you that our existence does not, like hers, enjoy an infinitely indicative mood, an eternally present tense, a limitlessly active voice, for in our shambling, slovenly makeshift world any two persons, whether domestic first or neighbourly second, require and necessarily presuppose in both their numbers and in all their cases, the whole inflected gamut of an alien third since, without a despised or dreaded Them to turn the back *on*, there could be no intimate or affectionate Us to turn the eye *to*; that, *chez nous*, space to never the whole uninhabited circle but always some segment, its eminent domain upheld by two co-ordinates There always has been and always will be not only the vertical boundary, the river on this side of which initiative and honesty stroll arm in arm wearing sensible clothes, and beyond which is a savage elsewhere swarming with contagious diseases, but also its horizontal counterpart, the railroad above which houses stand in their own grounds, each equipped with a garage and a beautiful woman, sometimes with several, and below which huddled shacks provide a squeezing shelter to collarless herds who eat blancmange and have never said anything witty. Make the case as special as you please; take the tamest congregation or the wildest faction; take, say, a college. What river and railroad did for the grosser instance, lawn and corridor do for the more refined, dividing the tender who value from the tough who measure, the superstitious who still sacrifice to causation from the heretics who have already reduced the worship of truth to bare description, and so creating the academic fields to be guarded with umbrella and learned periodical against the trespass of any unqualified stranger, not a whit less jealously than the game-preserve is protected from the poacher by the unamiable shot-gun. For without these prohibitive frontiers we should never know who we were or what we wanted. It is they who donate to neighbourhood all its accuracy and vehemence. It is thanks to them that we do know with whom to associate, make love, exchange recipes and jokes, go mountain climbing or sit side by side fishing from piers. It is thanks to them, too, that we know against whom to rebel. We *can* shock our parents by visiting the dives below the railroad tracks, we *can* amuse ourselves on what would otherwise have been a very dull evening indeed, in plotting to seize the post office across the river.

Of course these several private regions must together comprise one public whole—we would never deny that logic and instinct require that—of course. We and They are united in the candid glare of the same commercial hope by day, and the soft refulgence of the same erotic nostalgia by night—and this is our point—without our privacies of situation, our local idioms of triumph and mishap, our different doctrines concerning the transubstantiation of the larger pinker bun on the terrestrial dish for which the mature sense may reasonably water and the adult fingers furtively or unabashedly go for, our specific choices of which hill it would be romantic to fly away over or what sea it would be exciting to run away to, our peculiar visions of the absolute stranger with a spontaneous longing

37

for the lost who will adopt our misery not out of desire but pure compassion, without, in short, our devoted pungent expression of the partial and contrasted, the Whole would have no importance and its Day and Night no interest.

So, too, with Time who, in our auditorium, is not her dear old buffer so anxious to please everybody, but a prim magistrate whose court never adjourns, and from whose decisions, as he laconically sentences one to loss of hair and talent, another to seven days' chastity, and a third to boredom for life, there is no appeal. We should not be sitting here now, washed, warm, well-fed, in seats we have paid for, unless there were others who are not here; our liveliness and good-humour, such as they are, are those of survivors, conscious that there are others who have not been so fortunate, others who did not succeed in navigating the narrow passage or to whom the natives were not friendly, others whose streets were chosen by the explosion or through whose country the famine turned aside from ours to go, others who failed to repel the invasion of bacteria or to crush the insurrection of their bowels, others who lost their suit against their parents or were ruined by wishes they could not adjust or murdered by resentments they could not control; aware of some who were better and bigger but from whom, only the other day, Fortune withdrew her hand in sudden disgust, now nervously playing chess with drunken sea-captains in sordid cafés on the equator or the Arctic Circle, or lying, only a few blocks away, strapped and screaming on iron beds or dropping to naked pieces in damp graves. And shouldn't you too, dear master, reflect—forgive us for mentioning it—that we might very well not have been attending a production of yours this evening, had not some other and maybe—who can tell?—brighter talent married a barmaid or turned religious and shy or gone down in a liner with all his manuscripts, the loss recorded only in the corner of some country newspaper below A Poultry Lover's Jottings?

You yourself, we seem to remember, have spoken of the conjured spectacle as 'a mirror held up to nature', a phrase misleading in its aphoristic sweep but indicative at least of one aspect of the relation between the real and the imagined, their mutual reversal of value, for isn't the essential artistic strangeness to which your citation of the sinisterly biased image would point just this: that on the far side of the mirror the general will to compose, to form at all costs a felicitous pattern, becomes the *necessary cause* of any particular effort to live or act or love or triumph or vary, instead of being as, in so far as it emerges at all, it is on this side, their *accidental effect*?

Does Ariel—to nominate the spirit of reflection in your terms—call for manifestation? Then neither modesty nor fear of reprisals excuses the one so called on from publicly confessing that she cheated at croquet or that he committed incest in a dream. Does He demand concealment? Then their nearest and dearest must be deceived by disguises of sex and age which anywhere else would at once attract the attentions of the police or the derisive whistle of the awful schoolboy. That is the price asked, and how promptly and gladly paid, for universal reconciliation and peace, for the privilege of all galloping together past the finishing post neck and neck.

How then, we continue to wonder, knowing all this, could you act as if you did not, as if you did not realize that the embarrassing compresence of the absolutely natural, incorrigibly right-handed, and, to any request for co-operation, utterly negative, with the enthusiastically self-effacing would be a simultaneous violation of both worlds, as if you were not perfectly well aware that the magical musical condition, the orphic spell that turns the fierce dumb greedy beasts into grateful guides and oracles who will gladly take one anywhere and tell one everything free of charge, is precisely and simply that of his finite immediate note *not*, under any circumstances, being struck, of its

39

not being tentatively whispered, far less positively banged.

Are we not bound to conclude, then, that, whatever snub to the poetic you may have intended incidentally to administer, your profounder motive in so introducing Him to them among whom, because He doesn't belong, He couldn't appear as anything but His distorted parody, a deformed and savage slave, was to deal a mortal face-slapping insult to us among whom He does and is, moreover, all grossness turned to glory, no less a person than the nude august elated archer of our heaven, the darling single son of Her who, in her right milieu, is certainly no witch but the most sensible of all the gods, whose influence is as sound as it is pandemic, on the race-track no less than in the sleeping cars of the Orient Express, our great white Queen of Love herself?

But even that is not the worst we suspect you of. If your words have not buttered any parsnips, neither have they broken any bones.

He, after all, can come back to us now to be comforted and respected, perhaps, after the experience of finding himself for a few hours and for the first time in His life not wanted, more fully and freshly appreciative of our affection than He has always been in the past; as for His dear mother, She is far too grand and far too busy to hear or care what you say or think. If only we were certain that your malice was confined to the verbal affront, we should long ago have demanded our money back and gone whistling home to bed. Alas, in addition to resenting what you have openly said, we fear even more what you may secretly have done. Is it possible that, not content with inveigling Caliban into Ariel's kingdom, you have also let loose Ariel in Caliban's? We note with alarm that when the other members of the final tableau were dismissed, He was not returned to His arboreal confinement as He should have been. Where is He now? For if the intrusion of the real has disconcerted and incommoded the poetic, that is a mere bagatelle compared to the damage which the poetic would inflict if it ever succeeded in intruding upon the real. We want no Ariel here, breaking down our picket fences in the name of fraternity, seducing our wives in the name of romance, and robbing us of our sacred pecuniary deposits in the name of justice. Where is Ariel? What have you done with Him? For we won't, we daren't leave until you give us a satisfactory answer.

Such (let me cease to play your echo and return to my officially natural role)—such are your questions, are they not, but before I try to deal with them, I must ask for your patience, while I deliver a special message for our late author to those few among you, if indeed there be any—I have certainly heard no comment yet from them—who have come here, not to be entertained but to learn; that is, to any gay apprentice in the magical art who may have chosen this specimen of the prestidigatory genus to study this evening in the hope of grasping more clearly just how the artistic contraption works, of observing some fresh detail in the complex process by which the heady wine of amuse-ment is distilled from the grape of composition. The rest of you I must beg for a little while to sit back and relax as the remarks I have now to make do not concern you; your turn will follow later.

So, strange young man,—it is at his command, remem-ber, that I say this to you; whether I agree with it or not is neither here nor there—you have decided on the conjurer's profession. Somewhere, in the middle of a salt marsh or at the bottom of a kitchen garden or on the top of a bus, you heard imprisoned Ariel call for help, and it is now a liber-ator's face that congratulates you from your shaving mirror every morning. As you walk the cold streets hatless, or sit over coffee and doughnuts in the corner of a cheap restaurant, your secret has already set you apart from the howling merchants and transacting multitudes to watch with fascinated distaste the bellowing barging banging

41

passage of the awkward profit-seeking elbow, the dazed eye of the gregarious acquisitive condition. Lying awake at night in your single bed you are conscious of a power by which you will survive the wallpaper of your boardinghouse or the expensive bourgeois horrors of your home. Yes, Ariel is grateful; He does come when you call, He does tell you all the gossip He overhears on the stairs, all the goings-on He observes through the keyhole; he really is willing to arrange anything you care to ask for, and you are rapidly finding out the right orders to give—who should be killed in the hunting accident, which couple to send into the cast-iron shelter, what scent will arouse a Norwegian engineer, how to get the young hero from the country lawyer's office to the Princess's reception, when to mislay the letter, where the cabinet minister should be reminded of his mother, why the dishonest valet must be a martyr to indigestion but immune from the common cold.

As the gay productive months slip by, in spite of fretful discouraged days, of awkward moments of misunderstanding or rather, seen retrospectively as happily cleared up and got over, verily because of them, you are definitely getting the hang of this, at first so novel and bewildering, relationship between magician and familiar, whose duty it is to sustain your infinite conceptual appetite with vivid concrete experiences. And, as the months turn into years, your wonder-working romance into an economical habit, the encountered case of good or evil in our wide world of property and boredom which leaves you confessedly and unsympathetically at a loss, the aberrant phase in the whole human cycle of ecstasy and exhaustion with which you are imperfectly familiar, become increasingly rare. No perception however petite, no notion however subtle, escapes your attention or baffles your understanding: on entering any room you immediately distinguish the wasters who throw away their fruit half-eaten from the preservers who bottle all the summer; as the passengers file down the ship's gangway you unerringly guess which suitcase contains indecent novels; a five-minute chat about the weather or the coming elections is all you require to diagnose any distemper, however self-assured, for by then your eye has already spotted the tremor of the lips in that infinitesimal moment while the lie was getting its balance, your ear all ready picked up the heart's low whimper which the capering legs were determined to stifle, your nose detected on love's breath the trace of ennui which foretells his early death, or the despair just starting to smoulder at the base of the scholar's brain which years hence will suddenly blow it up with one appalling laugh: in every case you can prescribe the saving treatment called for, knowing at once when it may be gentle and remedial when all that is needed is soft music and a pretty girl, and when it must be drastic and surgical, when nothing will do any good but political disgrace or financial and erotic failure. If I seem to attribute these powers to you when the eyes, the ears, the nose, the putting two and two together are, of course, all His, and yours only the primitive wish to know, it is a rhetorical habit I have caught from your, in the main juvenile and feminine, admirers whose naive unawareness of whom they ought properly to thank and praise you see no point in, for mere accuracy's stuffy sake, correcting.

Anyway, the partnership is a brilliant success. On you go together to ever greater and faster triumphs; ever more major grows the accumulated work, ever more masterly the manner, sound even at its pale sententious worst, and at its best the rich red personal flower of the grave and grand, until one day which you can never either at the time or later identify exactly, your strange fever reaches its crisis and from now on begins, ever so slowly, maybe to subside. At first you cannot tell what or why is the matter; you have only a vague feeling that it is no longer between you so smooth and sweet as it used to be. Sour silences appear, at first only for an occasional moment, but progressively more frequently and more prolonged, curdled moods in which you cannot for the life of you think of any request to make, and His dumb standing around, waiting for orders gets inexplicably but maddeningly on your nerves, until presently, to your amazement, you hear yourself asking Him if He wouldn't like a vacation and are shocked by your feeling of intense disappointment when He who has always hitherto so immediately and recklessly taken your slightest hint, says gauchely 'No.' So it goes on from exasperated bad to desperate worst until you realize in despair that there is nothing for it but you two to part. Collecting all your strength for the distasteful task, you finally manage to stammer or shout 'You are free. Goodbye,' but to your dismay He whose obedience through all the enchanted years has never been less than perfect, now refuses to budge. Striding up to Him in fury, you glare into His unblinking eyes and stop dead, transfixed with horror at seeing reflected there, not what you had always expected to see, a conqueror smiling at a conqueror, both promising mountains and marvels, but a gibbering fist-clenched creature with which you are all too unfamiliar, for this is the first time indeed that you have met the only subject that you have, who is not a dream amenable to magic but the all too solid flesh you must acknowledge as your own; at last you have come face to face with me, and are appalled to learn how far I am from being, in any sense, your dish; how completely lacking in that poise and calm and all forgiving because all understanding good nature which to the critical eye is so wonderfully and domestically present on every page of your published inventions.

But where, may I ask, should I have acquired them, when, like a society mother who, although she is, of course, as she tells everyone, absolutely *devoted* to her child, simply *cannot* leave the dinner table just now and really *must* be in Le Touquet tomorrow, and so leaves him in charge of servants she doesn't know or boarding schools she has never seen, you have never in all these years taken the faintest personal interest in me? 'Oh!' you protestingly gasp, 'but how can you say such a thing, after I've toiled and moiled and worked my fingers to the bone, trying to give you a good home, after all the hours I've spent planning wholesome nourishing meals for you, after all the things I've gone without so that you should have swimming lessons and piano lessons and a new bicycle. Have I ever let you go out in summer without your sun hat, or come in in winter without feeling your stockings and insisting, if they were the least bit damp, on your changing them at once? Haven't you always been allowed to do everything, in reason, that you liked?'

Exactly: even deliberate ill-treatment would have been less unkind. Gallows and battlefields are, after all, no less places of mutual concern than sofa and bridal-bed; the dashing flirtations of fighter pilots and the coy tactics of twirled moustache and fluttered fan, the gasping mud-caked wooing of the coarsest foes and the reverent rage of the highest-powered romance, the lover's nip and the grip of the torturer's tongs are all,—ask Ariel,—variants of one common type, the bracket within which life and death with such passionate gusto cohabit, to be distinguished solely by the plus or minus sign which stands before them, signs which He is able at any time and in either direction to switch, but the one exception, the sum no magic of His can ever transmute, is the indifferent zero. Had you tried to destroy me, had we wrestled through long dark hours, we might by daybreak have learnt something from each other; in some panting pause to recover breath for further more savage blows or in the moment before your death or mine, we might both have heard together that music which explains and pardons all.

Had you, on the other hand, really left me alone to go my whole free-wheeling way to disorder, to be drunk every day before lunch, to jump stark naked from bed to bed, to have a fit every week or a major operation every other year, to forge cheques or water the widow's stock, I might, after countless skids and punctures, have come by the bumpy third-class road of guilt and remorse, smack into that very same truth which you were meanwhile admiring from your distant comfortable veranda but would never point out to me.

Such genuine escapades, though, might have disturbed the master at his meditations and even involved him in trouble with the police. The strains of oats, therefore, that you prudently permitted me to sow were each and all of an unmitigatedly minor wildness: a quick cold clasp now and then in some *louche* hotel to calm me down while you got on with the so thorough documentation of your great unhappy love for one who by being bad or dead or married provided you with the Good Right Subject that would never cease to bristle with importance; one bout of flu per winter, an occasional twinge of toothache, and enough tobacco to keep me in a good temper while you composed your melting eclogues of rustic piety; licence to break my shoelaces, spill soup on my tie, burn cigarette holes in the tablecloth, lose letters and borrowed books, and generally keep myself busy while you polished to a perfection your lyric praises of the more candid, more luxurious world to come.

Can you wonder then, when, as was bound to happen sooner or later, your charms, because they no longer amuse you, have cracked and your spirits, because you are tired of giving orders, have ceased to obey, and you are left alone with me, the dark thing you could never abide to be with, if I do not yield you kind answer or admire you for the achievements I was never allowed to profit from, if I resent hearing you speak of your neglect of me as your 'exile', of the pains you never took with me as 'all lost'?

But why continue? From now on we shall have, as we both know only too well, no company but each other's,

46

and if I have had, as I consider, a good deal to put up with from you, I must own that, after all, I am not just the person I would have chosen for a life companion myself; so the only chance, which in any case is slim enough, of my getting a tolerably new master and you a tolerably new man, lies in our both learning, if possible and as soon as possible, to forgive and forget the past, and to keep our respective hopes for the future, within moderate, very moderate limits.

And now at last it is you, assorted, consorted specimens of the general popular type, the major flock who have trotted trustingly hither but found, you reproachfully baah, no grazing, that I turn to and address on behalf of Ariel and myself. To your questions I shall attempt no direct reply, for the mere fact that you have been able so anxiously to put them is in itself sufficient proof that you possess their answers. All your clamour signifies is this: that your first big crisis, the breaking of the childish spell in which, so long as it enclosed you, there was, for you, no mirror, no magic, for everything that happened was a miracle it was just as extraordinary for a chair to be a chair as for it to turn into a horse; it was no more absurd that the girding on of coal-scuttle and poker should transform you into noble Hector than that you should have a father and mother who called you Tommy—and it was therefore only necessary for you to presuppose one genius, one unrivalled I to wish these wonders in all their endless plentitude and novelty to be, is, in relation to you present, behind, that your singular transparent globes of enchantment have shattered one by one, and you have now all come together in the larger colder emptier room on this side of the mirror which *does* force your eyes to recognize and reckon with the two of us, your ears to detect the irreconcilable difference between my reiterated affirmation of what your furnished circumstances categorically are, and His successive propositions as to everything else which

47

they conditionally might be. You have, as I say, taken your first step.

The journey of life—the down-at-heels disillusioned figure can still put its characterization across—is infinitely long and its possible destinations infinitely distant from one another, but the time spent in actual travel is infinitesimally small. The hours the traveller measures are those in which he is at rest between the three or four decisive instants of transportation which are all he needs and all he gets to carry him the whole of his way; the scenery he observes is the view, gorgeous or drab, he glimpses from platform to siding; the incidents he thrills or blushes to remember take place in waiting and wash-rooms, ticket queues and parcels offices: it is in those promiscuous places of random association, in that air of anticipatory fidget, that he makes friends and enemies, that he promises, confesses, kisses, and betrays until, either because it is the one he has been expecting, or because, losing his temper, he has vowed to take the first to come along, or because he has been given a free ticket, or simply by misdirection or mistake, a train arrives which he does get into: it whistles—at least he thinks afterwards he remembers it whistling—but before he can blink, it has come to a standstill again and there he stands clutching his battered bags, surrounded by entirely strange smells and noises—yet in their smelliness and noisiness how familiar—one vast important stretch the nearer Nowhere, that still smashed terminus at which he will, in due course, be deposited, seedy and by himself.

Yes, you have made a definite start; you *have* left your homes way back in the farming provinces or way out in the suburban tundras, but whether you have been hanging around for years or have barely and breathlessly got here on one of those locals which keep arriving minute after minute, this is still only the main depot, the Grandly Average Place from which at odd hours the expresses leave seriously and sombrely for Somewhere, and where it is still

48

possible for me to posit the suggestion that you go no farther. You will never, after all, feel better than in your present shaved and breakfasted state which there are restaurants and barber shops here indefinitely to preserve; you will never feel more secure than you do now in your knowledge that you *have* your ticket, your passport *is* in order, you have *not* forgotten to pack your pyjamas and an extra clean shirt; you will never have the same opportunity of learning about *all* the holy delectable spots of current or historic interest—an insistence on reaching *one* will necessarily exclude the others—than you have in these bepostered halls; you will never meet a jollier, more various crowd than you see around you here, sharing with you the throbbing, suppressed excitement of those to whom the exciting thing is still, perhaps, to happen. But once you leave, no matter in which direction, your next stop will be far outside this land of habit that so democratically stands up for your right to stagestruck hope, and well inside one of those, all equally foreign, uncomfortable and despotic, certainties of failure or success. Here at least I, and Ariel too, are free to warn you not, should we meet again there, to speak to either of us, not to engage either of us as your guide, but there we shall no longer be able to refuse you; then, unfortunately for you, we shall be compelled to say nothing and obey your fatal foolish commands. Here, whether you listen to me or not, and it's highly improbable that you will, I can at least warn you what will happen if at our next meeting you should insist—and that is all too probable, on putting one of us in charge.

'Release us,' you will beg, then, supposing it is I whom you make for,—oh how awfully uniform, once one translates them out of your private lingoes of expression, all your sorrows are and how awfully well I know them—'release us from our minor roles. Carry me back, Master, to the cathedral town where the canons run through the water meadows with butterfly nets and the old women keep sweet-shops in the cobbled side streets, or back to the upland mill town (gunpowder and plush) with its grope-movie and its pool-room lit by gas, carry me back to the days before my wife had put on weight, back to the years when beer was cheap and the rivers really froze in winter. Pity me, Captain, pity a poor old stranded sea-salt whom an unlucky voyage has wrecked on the desolate mahogany coast of this bar with nothing left him but his big moustache. Give me my passage home, let me see that harbour once again just as it was before I learned the bad words. Patriarchs wiser than Abraham mended their nets on the modest wharf; white and wonderful beings undressed on the sand-dunes; sunset glittered on the plate-glass windows of the Marine Biological Station; far off on the extreme horizon a whale spouted. Look, Uncle, look. They have broken my glasses and I have lost my silver whistle. Pick me up, Uncle, let little Johnny ride away on your massive shoulders to recover his green kingdom, where the steam rollers are as friendly as the farm dogs and it would never become necessary to look over one's left shoulder or clench one's right fist in one's pocket. You cannot miss it. Black currant bushes hide the ruined opera house where badgers are said to breed in great numbers; an old horse-tramway winds away westward through suave foothills crowned with stone circles—follow it and by nightfall one would come to a large good-natured waterwheel—to the north, beyond a forest inhabited by charcoal burners, one can see the Devil's Bedposts quite distinctly, to the east the museum where for sixpence one can touch the ivory chessmen. O Cupid, Cupid, howls the whole dim chorus, take us home. We have never felt really well in this climate of distinct ideas; we have never been able to follow the regulations properly; Business, Science, Religion, Art, and all the other fictitious immortal persons who matter here have, frankly, not been very kind. We're so, so tired, the rewarding soup is stone cold, and over our blue wonders the grass grew

50

long ago. O take us home with you, strong and swelling One, home to your promiscuous pastures where the minotaur of authority is just a roly-poly ruminant and nothing is at stake, those purring sites and amusing vistas where the fluctuating arabesques of sound, the continuous eruption of colours and scents, the whole rich incoherence of a nature made up of gaps and asymetrical events plead beautifully and bravely for our undistress.'

And in that very moment when you so cry for deliverance from any and every anxious possibility, I shall have no option but to be faithful to my oath of service and instantly transport you, not indeed to any cathedral town or mill town or harbour or hillside or jungle or other specific Eden which your memory necessarily but falsely conceives of as the ultimately liberal condition, which in point of fact you have never known yet, but directly to that downright state itself. Here you are. This is it. Directly overhead a full moon casts a circle of dazzling light without any penumbra, exactly circumscribing its desolation in which every object is extraordinarily still and sharp. Cones of extinct volcanoes rise up abruptly from the lava plateau fissured by chasms and pitted with hot springs from which steam rises without interruption straight up into the windless rarefied atmosphere. Here and there a geyser erupts without warning, spouts furiously for a few seconds and as suddenly subsides. Here, where the possessive note is utterly silent and all events are tautological repetitions and no decision will ever alter the secular stagnation, at long last you are, as you have asked to be, the only subject. Who, When, Why, the poor tired little historic questions fall wilting into a hush of utter failure. Your tears splash down upon clinkers which will never be persuaded to recognize a neighbour and there is really and truly no one to appear with tea and help. You have indeed come all the way to the end of your bachelor's journey where Liberty stands with her hands behind her back, not caring, not

51

minding *anything*. Confronted by a straight and snubbing stare to which mythology is bosh, surrounded by an infinite passivity and purely arithmetical disorder which is only open to perception, and with nowhere to go on to, your existence is indeed free at last to choose its own meaning, that is, to plunge headlong into despair and fall through silence fathomless and dry, all fact your single drop, all value your pure alas.

*　　　　　*　　　　　*

But what of that other, smaller but doubtless finer group among you, important persons at the top of the ladder, exhausted lions of the season, local authorities with their tense tired faces, elderly hermits of both sexes living gloomily in the delta of a great fortune, whose *amour propre* prefers to turn for help to my more spiritual colleague.

'O yes,' you will sigh, 'we have had what once we would have called success. I moved the vices out of the city into a chain of re-conditioned lighthouses. I introduced statistical methods into the Liberal Arts. I revived the country dances and installed electric stoves in the mountain cottages. I saved democracy by buying steel. I gave the caesura its freedom. But this world is no better and it is now quite clear to us that there is nothing to be done with such a ship of fools, adrift on a sugarloaf sea in which it is going very soon and suitably to founder. Deliver us, dear Spirit, from the tantrums of our telephones and the whispers of our secretaries conspiring against Man; deliver us from these helpless agglomerations of dishevelled creatures with their bed-wetting, vomiting, weeping bodies, their giggling, fugitive, disappointing hearts, and scrawling, blotted, misspelt minds, to whom we have so foolishly tried to bring the light they did not want; deliver us from all the litter of *billets-doux*, empty beer bottles, laundry lists, directives, promissory notes and broken toys, the terrible mess that this particularized life, which we have so futilely attempted to tidy, sullenly insists on leaving behind it; translate us, bright Angel, from this hell of inert and ailing matter, growing steadily senile in a time for ever immature, to that blessed realm, so far above the twelve impertinent winds and the four unreliable seasons, that Heaven of the Really General Case where, tortured no longer by three dimensions and immune from temporal vertigo, Life turns into Light, absorbed for good into the permanently stationary, completely self-sufficient, absolutely reasonable One.'

Obliged by the terms of His contract to gratify this other request of yours, the wish for freedom to transcend *any* condition, for direct unentailed power without *any*, however secretly immanent, obligation to inherit or transmit, what can poor shoulder-shrugging Ariel do but lead you forthwith into a nightmare which has all the wealth of exciting action and all the emotional poverty of an adventure story for boys, a state of perpetual emergency and everlasting inprovisation where all is need and change.

All the phenomena of an empirically ordinary world are given. Extended objects appear to which events happen— old men catch dreadful coughs, little girls get their arms twisted, flames run whooping through woods, round a river bend, as harmless looking as a dirty old bearskin rug, comes the gliding fury of a town-effacing wave, but these are merely elements in an allegorical landscape to which mathematical measurement and phenomenological analysis have no relevance.

All the voluntary movements are possible—crawling through flues and old sewers, sauntering past shop-fronts, tiptoeing through quicksands and mined areas, running through derelict factories and across empty plains, jumping over brooks, diving into pools or swimming along between banks of roses, pulling at manholes or pushing at revolving doors, clinging to rotten balustrades, sucking at straws or wounds; all the modes of transport, letters, ox-carts, canoes, hansom cabs, trains, trolleys, cars, aeroplanes, balloons, are available, but any sense of direction,

53

any knowledge of where on earth one has come from or where on earth one is going to is completely absent.

Religion and culture seem to be represented by a catholic belief that something is lacking which must be found, but as to what that something is, the keys of heaven, the missing heir, genius, the smells of childhood, or a sense of humour, why it is lacking, whether it has been deliberately stolen, or accidentally lost or just hidden for a lark, and who is responsible, our ancestors, ourselves, the social structure, or mysterious wicked powers, there are as many faiths as there are searchers, and clues can be found behind every clock, under every stone, and in every hollow tree to support all of them.

Again, other selves undoubtedly exist, but though everyone's pocket is bulging with birth certificates, insurance policies, passports and letters of credit, there is no way of proving whether they are genuine or planted or forged, so that no one knows whether another is his friend disguised as an enemy or his enemy disguised as a friend (there is probably no one whose real name is Brown), or whether the police who here as elsewhere are grimly busy, are crushing a criminal revolt or upholding a vicious tyranny, any more than he knows whether he himself is a victim of the theft, or the thief, or a rival thief, a professionally interested detective or a professionally impartial journalist.

Even the circumstances of the tender passion, the long-distance calls, the assignation at the aquarium, the farewell embrace under the fish-tail burner on the landing, are continually present, but since, each time it goes through its performance, it never knows whether it is saving a life, or obtaining secret information, or forgetting or spiting its real love, the heart feels nothing but a dull percussion of conceptional foreboding. Everything, in short, suggests Mind but, surrounded by an infinite extension of the adolescent difficulty, a rising of the subjective and subjunctive

54

to ever steeper, stormier heights, the panting frozen expressive gift has collapsed under the strain of its communicative anxiety, and contributes nothing by way of meaning but a series of staccato barks or a delirious gush of glossolalia.

And from this nightmare of public solitude, this everlasting Not Yet, what relief have you but in an ever giddier collective gallop, with bisson eye and bevel course, toward the gray horizon of the bleaker vision, what landmarks but the four dead rivers, the Joyless, the Flaming, the Mournful, and the Swamp of Tears, what goal but the black stone on which the bones are cracked, for only there in its cry of agony can your existence find at last an unequivocal meaning and your refusal to be yourself become a serious despair, the love nothing, the fear all?

*   *   *

Such are the alternative routes, the facile glad-handed highway or the virtuous averted track, by which the human effort to make its own fortune arrives all eager at its abruptly dreadful end. I have tried—the opportunity was not to be neglected—to raise the admonitory forefinger, to ring the alarming bell, but with so little confidence of producing the right result, so certain that the open eye and attentive ear will always interpret any sight and any sound to their advantage, every rebuff as a consolation, every prohibition as a rescue—that is what they open and attend for—that I find myself almost hoping, for your sake, that I have had the futile honour of addressing the blind and the deaf.

Having learnt his language, I begin to feel something of the serio-comic embarrassment of the dedicated dramatist, who, in representing to you your condition of estrangement from the truth, is doomed to fail the more he succeeds, for the more truthfully he paints the condition, the less clearly can he indicate the truth from which it is estranged, the brighter his revelation of the truth in its

55

order, its justice, its joy, the fainter shows his picture of your actual condition in all its drabness and sham, and, worse still, the more sharply he defines the estrangement itself—and, ultimately, what other aim and justification has he, what else exactly *is* the artistic gift which he is forbidden to hide, if not to make you unforgettably conscious of the ungarnished offended gap between what you so questionably are and what you are commanded without any question to become, of the unqualified No that opposes your every step in any direction?—the more he must strengthen your delusion that an awareness of the gap is in itself a bridge, your interest in your imprisonment a release, so that, far from your being led by him to contrition and surrender, the regarding of your defects in his mirror, your dialogue, using his words, with yourself about yourself, becomes the one activity which never, like devouring or collecting or spending, lets you down, the one game which can be guaranteed, whatever the company, to catch on, a madness of which you can only be cured by some shock quite outside his control, an unpredictable misting over of his glass or an absurd misprint in his text.

Our unfortunate dramatist, therefore, is placed in the unseemly predicament of having to give all his passion, all his skill, all his time to the task of 'doing' life—consciously to give anything less than all would be a gross betrayal of his gift and an unpardonable presumption—as if it lay in *his* power to solve this dilemma—yet of having at the same time to hope that some unforeseen mishap will intervene to ruin his effect, without, however, obliterating your disappointment, the expectation aroused by him that there was an effect to ruin, that, if the smiling interest never did arrive, it must, through no fault of its own, have got stuck somewhere; that, exhausted, ravenous, delayed by fog, mobbed and mauled by a thousand irrelevancies, it has, nevertheless, not forgotten its promise but is still trying desperately to get a connection.

56

Beating about for some large loose image to define the original drama which aroused his imitative passion, the first performance in which the players were their own audience, the worldly stage on which their behaving flesh was really sore and sorry—for the floods of tears were not caused by onions, the deformities and wounds did not come off after a good wash, the self-stabbed heroine could not pick herself up again to make a gracious bow nor her seducer go demurely home to his plain and middle-aged spouse—the fancy immediately flushed is of the greatest grandest opera rendered by a very provincial touring company indeed.

Our performance—for Ariel and I are, you know this now, just as deeply involved as any of you—which we were obliged, all of us, to go on with and sit through right to the final dissonant chord, has been so indescribably inexcusably awful. Sweating and shivering in our moth-eaten ill-fitting stock costumes which with only a change of hat and re-arrangement of safety-pins, had to do for the *landsknecht* and the Parisian art-student, bumping into, now a rippling palace, now a primeval forest full of holes, at cross purposes with the scraping bleating orchestra we could scarcely hear for half the instruments were missing and the cottage piano which was filling-out must have stood for too many years in some damp parlour, we floundered on from fiasco to fiasco, the schmalz tenor never quite able at his big moments to get right up nor the ham bass right down, the stud contralto gargling through her maternal grief, the ravished coloratura trilling madly off-key and the re-united lovers half a bar apart, the knock-kneed armies shuffling limply through their bloody battles, the unearthly harvesters hysterically entangled in their honest fugato.

Now it is over. No, we have not dreamt it. Here we really stand, down stage with red faces and no applause; no effect, however simple, no piece of business, however unimportant, came off; there was not a single aspect of our whole production, not even the huge stuffed bird of happiness, for which a kind word could, however patronizingly, be said.

Yet, at this very moment when we do at last see ourselves as we are, neither cosy nor playful, but swaying out on the ultimate wind-whipped cornice that overhangs the unabiding void—we have never stood anywhere else—, when our reasons are silenced by the heavy huge derision, —There is nothing to say. There never has been—, and our wills chuck in their hands—There is no way out. There never was—, it is at this moment that for the first time in our lives we hear, not the sounds which, as born actors, we have hitherto condescended to use as an excellent vehicle for displaying our personalities and looks, but the real Word which is our only *raison d'être*. Not that we have improved; everything, the massacres, the whippings, the lies, the twaddle, and all their carbon copies are still present, more obviously than ever; nothing has been reconstructed; our shame, our fear, our incorrigible staginess, all wish and no resolve, are still, and more intensely than ever, all we have: only now it is not in spite of them but with them that we are blessed by that Wholly Other Life from which we are separated by an essential emphatic gulf of which our contrived fissures of mirror and proscenium arch—we understand them at last—are feebly figurative signs, so that all our meanings are reversed and it is precisely in its negative image of Judgment that we can positively envisage Mercy; it is just here, among the ruins and the bones, that we may rejoice in the perfected Work which is not ours. Its great coherences stand out through our secular blur in all their overwhelmingly righteous obligation; its voice speaks through our muffling banks of artificial flowers and unflinchingly delivers its authentic molar pardon; its spaces greet us with all their grand old prospect of wonder and width; the working charm is the full bloom of the unbothered state; the sounded note is the restored relation.

POSTSCRIPT

(Ariel to Caliban. Echo by the Prompter

Weep no more but pity me,
Fleet persistent shadow cast
By your lameness, caught at last,
Helplessly in love with you,
Elegance, art, fascination,
   Fascinated by
   Drab mortality;
Spare me a humiliation,
   To your faults be true:
I can sing as you reply
        ...I

Wish for nothing lest you mar
The perfection in these eyes
Whose entire devotion lies
At the mercy of your will;
Tempt not your sworn comrade,—only
   As I am can I
   Love you as you are—
For my company be lonely
   For my health be ill:
I will sing if you will cry
        ...I

Never hope to say farewell,
For our lethargy is such
Heaven's kindness cannot touch
Nor earth's frankly brutal drum;
This was long ago decided,

Both of us know why,
    Can, alas, foretell,
When our falsehoods are divided,
    What we shall become,
One evaporating sigh
                    ... I

FOR THE TIME BEING

A Christmas Oratorio

IN MEMORIAM
CONSTANCE ROSALIE AUDEN
1870–1941

What shall we say then? Shall we continue in
sin, that grace may abound? God forbid.
ROMANS VI

ADVENT

I

CHORUS

Darkness and snow descend;
The clock on the mantelpiece
Has nothing to recommend,
Nor does the face in the glass
Appear nobler than our own
As darkness and snow descend
On all personality.
Huge crowds mumble—'Alas,
Our angers do not increase,
Love is not what she used to be';
Portly Caesar yawns—'I know';
He falls asleep on his throne,
They shuffle off through the snow:
Darkness and snow descend.

SEMI-CHORUS

Can great Hercules keep his
Extraordinary promise
To reinvigorate the Empire?

61

Utterly lost, he cannot
Even locate his task but
Stands in some decaying orchard
Or the irregular shadow
Of a ruined temple, aware of
Being watched from the horrid mountains
By fanatical eyes yet
Seeing no one at all, only hearing
The silence softly broken
By the poisonous rustle
Of famishing Arachne.

CHORUS

Winter completes an age
With its thorough levelling;
Heaven's tourbillions of rage
Abolish the watchman's tower
And delete the cedar grove.
As winter completes an age,
The eyes huddle like cattle, doubt
Seeps into the pores and power
Ebbs from the heavy signet ring;
The prophet's lantern is out
And gone the boundary stone,
Cold the heart and cold the stove,
Ice condenses on the bone:
Winter completes an age.

SEMI-CHORUS

Outside the civil garden
Of every day of love there
Crouches a wild passion
  To destroy and be destroyed.
O who to boast their power
Have challenged it to charge? Like

Wheat our souls are sifted
  And cast into the void.

The evil and armed draw near;
The weather smells of their hate
And the houses smell of our fear;
Death has opened his white eye
And the black hole calls the thief
As the evil and armed draw near.
Ravens alight on the wall,
Our plans have all gone awry,
The rains will arrive too late,
Our resourceful general
Fell down dead as he drank
And his horses died of grief,
Our navy sailed away and sank;
The evil and armed draw near.

II

NARRATOR

If, on account of the political situation,
There are quite a number of homes without roofs, and men
Lying about in the countryside neither drunk nor asleep,
If all sailings have been cancelled till further notice,
If it's unwise now to say much in letters, and if,
Under the subnormal temperatures prevailing,
The two sexes are at present the weak and the strong,
That is not at all unusual for this time of year.
If that were all we should know how to manage: Flood, fire,
The desiccation of grasslands, restraint of princes,
Piracy on the high seas, physical pain and fiscal grief,
These after all are our familiar tribulations,

And we have been through them all before, many, many
        times
As events which belong to the natural world where
The occupation of space is the real and final fact
And time turns round itself in an obedient circle,
They occur again and again but only to pass
Again and again into their formal opposites,
From sword to ploughshare, coffin to cradle, war to work,
So that, taking the bad with the good, the pattern com-
        posed
By the ten thousand odd things that can possibly happen
Is permanent in a general average way.

    Till lately we knew of no other, and between us we
        seemed
To have what it took—the adrenal courage of the tiger,
The chameleon's discretion, the modesty of the doe,
Or the fern's devotion to spatial necessity:
To practise one's peculiar civic virtue was not
So impossible after all; to cut our losses
And bury our dead was really quite easy: That was why
We were always able to say: 'We are children of God,
And our Father has never forsaken His people.'

    But then we were children: That was a moment ago,
Before an outrageous novelty had been introduced
Into our lives. Why were we never warned? Perhaps we
        were.
Perhaps that mysterious noise at the back of the brain
We noticed on certain occasions—sitting alone
In the waiting room of the country junction, looking
Up at the toilet window—was not indigestion
But this Horror starting already to scratch Its way in?
Just how, just when It succeeded we shall never know:
We can only say that now It is there and that nothing
We learnt before It was there is now of the slightest use,

For nothing like it has happened before. It's as if
We had left our house for five minutes to mail a letter
And during that time the living room had changed places
With the room behind the mirror over the fireplace;
It's as if, waking up with a start, we discovered
Ourselves stretched out flat on the floor, watching our
        shadow
Sleepily stretching itself at the window. I mean
That the world of space where events reoccur is still there,
Only now it's no longer real; the real one is nowhere
Where time never moves and nothing can ever happen:
I mean that although there's a person we know all about
Still bearing our name and loving himself as before,
That person has become a fiction; our true existence
Is decided by no one and has no importance to love.

   That is why we despair; that is why we would welcome
The nursery bogey or the winecellar ghost, why even
The violent howling of winter and war has become
Like a juke-box tune that we dare not stop. We are afraid
Of pain but more afraid of silence; for no nightmare
Of hostile objects could be as terrible as this Void.
This is the Abomination. This is the wrath of God.

III

CHORUS

Alone, alone, about a dreadful wood
Of conscious evil runs a lost mankind,
Dreading to find its Father lest it find
The Goodness it has dreaded is not good:
Alone, alone, about our dreadful wood.

Where is that Law for which we broke our own,
Where now that Justice for which Flesh resigned
Her hereditary right to passion, Mind

His will to absolute power? Gone. Gone.
Where is that Law for which we broke our own?

The Pilgrim Way has led to the Abyss.
Was it to meet such grinning evidence
We left our richly odoured ignorance?
Was the triumphant answer to be this?
The Pilgrim Way has led to the Abyss.

We who must die demand a miracle.
How could the Eternal do a temporal act,
The Infinite become a finite fact?
Nothing can save us that is possible:
We who must die demand a miracle.

IV

RECITATIVE

If the muscle can feel repugnance, there is still a false move
     to be made;
If the mind can imagine tomorrow, there is still a defeat to
     remember;
As long as the self can say 'I', it is impossible not to rebel;
As long as there is an accidental virtue, there is a necessary
     vice:
And the garden cannot exist, the miracle cannot occur.

For the garden is the only place there is, but you will not
     find it
Until you have looked for it everywhere and found nowhere
     that is not a desert;
The miracle is the only thing that happens, but to you it
     will not be apparent,
Until all events have been studied and nothing happens
     that you cannot explain;
And life is the destiny you are bound to refuse until you
     have consented to die.

Therefore, see without looking, hear without listening,
    breathe without asking:
The Inevitable is what will seem to happen to you purely
    by chance;
The Real is what will strike you as really absurd;
Unless you are certain you are dreaming, it is certainly a
    dream of your own;
Unless you exclaim—'There must be some mistake'—you
    must be mistaken.

V

CHORUS

O where is that immortal and nameless Centre from which
    our points of
Definition and death are all equi-distant? Where
The well of our wish to wander, the everlasting fountain
    Of the waters of joy that our sorrow uses for tears?
O where is the garden of Being that is only known in Exist-
    ence
    As the command to be never there, the sentence by which
Alephs of throbbing fact have been banished into position,
    The clock that dismisses the moment into the turbine of
    time?

O would I could mourn over Fate like the others, the re-
    solute creatures,
    By seizing my chance to regret. The stone is content
With a formal anger and falls and falls; the plants are in-
    dignant
    With one dimension only and can only doubt
Whether light or darkness lies in the worse direction; and
    the subtler
    Exiles who try every path are satisfied
With proving that none have a goal: why must Man also
    acknowledge

67

It is not enough to bear witness, for even protest is
    wrong?

Earth is cooled and fire is quenched by his unique excite-
    ment,
    All answers expire in the clench of his questioning hand,
His singular emphasis frustrates all possible order:
    Alas, his genius is wholly for envy; alas,
The vegetative sadness of lakes, the locomotive beauty
    Of choleric beasts of prey, are nearer than he
To the dreams that deprive him of sleep, the powers that
    compel him to idle,
    To his amorous nymphs and his sanguine athletic gods.

How can his knowledge protect his desire for truth from
    illusion?
    How can he wait without idols to worship, without
Their overwhelming persuasion that somewhere, over the
    high hill,
    Under the roots of the oak, in the depths of the sea,
Is a womb or a tomb wherein he may halt to express some
    attainment?
    How can he hope and not dream that his solitude
Shall disclose a vibrating flame at last and entrust him for-
    ever
    With its magic secret of how to extemporize life?

THE ANNUNCIATION

I

THE FOUR FACULTIES

Over the life of Man
We watch and wait
The Four who manage
His fallen estate:
We who are four were
Once but one,
Before his act of
Rebellion;
We were himself when
His will was free,
His error became our
Chance to be.

Powers of air and fire,
Water and earth,
Into our hands is given
Man from his birth:

INTUITION

As a dwarf in the dark of
His belly I rest;

FEELING

A nymph, I inhabit
The heart in his breast;

SENSATION

A giant, at the gates of
His body I stand;

69

THOUGHT

His dreaming brain is
My fairyland.

TUTTI

Invisible phantoms,
The forms we assume are
Adapted to each
Individual humour,
Beautiful facts or true
Generalizations,
Test cases in Law or
Market quotations:
As figures and formulae
Chemists have seen us,
Who to true lovers were
Putti of Venus.

Ambiguous causes
Of all temptation,
We lure men either
To death or salvation:
We alone may look over
The wall of that hidden
Garden whose entrance
To him is forbidden;
Must truthfully tell him
What happens inside,
But what it may mean he
Alone must decide.

II

THOUGHT

The garden is unchanged, the silence is unbroken.
Truth has not yet intruded to possess

70

Its empty morning nor the promised hour
Shaken its lasting May.

INTUITION
The human night,
Whose messengers we are, cannot dispel
Its wanton dreams, and they are all we know.

SENSATION
My senses are still coarse
From late engrossment in a fair. Old tunes
Reiterated, lights with repeated winks,
Were fascinating like a tie and brought
Whole populations running to a plain,
Making its lush alluvial meadows
One boisterous preposter. By the river
A whistling crowd had waited many hours
To see a naked woman swim upstream;
Honours and reckless medicines were served
In booths where interest was lost
As easily as money; at the back,
In a wet vacancy among the ash cans,
A waiter coupled sadly with a crow.

FEELING
I have but now escaped a raging landscape:
There woods were in a tremor from the shouts
Of hunchbacks hunting a hermaphrodite;
A burning village scampered down a lane;
Insects with ladders stormed a virgin's house;
On a green knoll littered with picnics
A mob of horses kicked a gull to death.

71

INTUITION

Remembrance of the moment before last
Is like a yawning drug. I have observed
The sombre valley of an industry
In dereliction. Conduits, ponds, canals,
Distressed with weeds; engines and furnaces
At rust in rotting sheds; and ther strong users
Transformed to spongy heaps of drunken flesh.
Deep among dock and dusty nettle lay
Each ruin of a will; manors of mould
Grew into empires as a westering sun
Left the air chilly; not a sound disturbed
The autumn dusk except a stertorous snore
That over their drowned condition like a sea
Wept without grief.

THOUGHT

       My recent company
Was worse than your three visions. Where I was,
The haunting ghosts were figures with no ground,
Areas of wide omission and vast regions
Of passive colour; higher than any squeak,
One note went on for ever; an embarrassed sum
Stuck on the stutter of a decimal,
And points almost coincident already
Approached so slowly they could never meet.
There nothing could be stated or constructed:
To Be was an archaic nuisance.

INTUITION

Look. There is someone in the garden.

FEELING

The garden is unchanged, the silence is unbroken
For she is still walking in her sleep of childhood:

Many before
Have wandered in, like her, then wandered out
Unconscious of their visit and unaltered,
The garden unchanged, the silence unbroken:
None may wake there but One who shall be woken.

THE ANGEL GABRIEL

Wake.

III

GABRIEL

Mary, in a dream of love
Playing as all children play,
For unsuspecting children may
Express in comic make-believe
The wish that later they will know
Is tragic and impossible;
Hear, child, what I am sent to tell:
Love will your dream to happen, so
Love's will on earth may be, through you,
No longer a pretend but true.

MARY

What dancing joy would whirl
My ignorance away?
Light blazes out of the stone,
The taciturn water
Burst into music,
And warm wings throb within
The motionless rose:
What sudden rush of Power
Commands me to command?

73

GABRIEL

When Eve, in love with her own will,
Denied the will of Love and fell,
She turned the flesh Love knew so well
To knowledge of her love until
Both love and knowledge were of sin:
What her negation wounded, may
Your affirmation heal today;
Love's will requires your own, that in
The flesh whose love you do not know,
Love's knowledge into flesh may grow.

MARY

My flesh in terror and fire
Rejoices that the Word
Who utters the world out of nothing,
As a pledge of His word to love her
Against her will, and to turn
Her desperate longing to love,
Should ask to wear me,
From now to their wedding day,
For an engagement ring.

GABRIEL

Since Adam, being free to choose,
Chose to imagine he was free
To choose his own necessity,
Lost in his freedom, Man pursues
The shadow of his images:
Today the Unknown seeks the known;
What I am willed to ask, your own
Will has no answer; child, it lies
Within your power of choosing to
Conceive the Child who chooses you.

74

IV

Let number and weight rejoice
In this hour of their translation
Into conscious happiness:
For the whole in every part,
The truth at the proper centre
(*There's a Way. There's a Voice.*)
Of language and distress
Is recognized in her heart
Singing and dancing.

Let even the great rejoice.
Though buffeted by admirers
And arrogant as noon,
The rich and the lovely have seen
For an infinitesimal moment
(*There's a Way. There's a Voice.*)
In another's eye till their own
Reflection came between,
Singing and dancing.

Let even the small rejoice
Though threatened from purple rostra
And dazed by the soldier's drum
Proclaiming total defeat,
The general loquacious Public
(*There's a Way. There's a Voice.*)
Have been puzzled and struck dumb,
Hearing in every street
Singing and dancing.

Let even the young rejoice
Lovers at their betrayal
Weeping alone in the night,

75

Have fallen asleep as they heard,
Though too far off to be certain
(*There's a Way. There's a Voice.*)
They had not imagined it,
Sounds that made grief absurd,
Singing and dancing.

Let even the old rejoice
The Bleak and the Dim abandoned
By impulse and regret,
Are startled out of their lives;
For to footsteps long expected
(*There's a Way. There's a Voice.*)
Their ruins echo, yet
The Demolisher arrives
Singing and dancing.

THE TEMPTATION OF ST. JOSEPH

I

JOSEPH

My shoes were shined, my pants were cleaned
        and pressed,
And I was hurrying to meet
    My own true Love:
But a great crowd grew and grew
Till I could not push my way through,
    Because
A star had fallen down the street;
    When they saw who I was,
The police tried to do their best.

CHORUS [*off*]

Joseph, you have heard
What Mary says occurred;
Yes, it may be so.
Is it likely? No.

JOSEPH

The bar was gay, the lighting well-designed,
And I was sitting down to wait
    My own true Love:
A voice I'd heard before, I think,
Cried: 'This is on the House. I drink
    To him
Who does not know it is too late';
    When I asked for the time,
Everyone was very kind.

Mary may be pure,
But, Joseph, are you sure?
How is one to tell?
Suppose, for instance . . . Well . . .

JOSEPH

Through cracks, up ladders, into waters deep,
I squeezed, I climbed, I swam to save
    My own true Love:
Under a dead apple tree
I saw an ass; when it saw me
    It brayed;
A hermit sat in the mouth of a cave;
    When I asked him the way,
He pretended to be asleep.

CHORUS [*off*]

Maybe, maybe not.
But, Joseph, you know what
Your world, of course, will say
About you anyway.

JOSEPH

Where are you, Father, where?
Caught in the jealous trap
Of an empty house I hear
As I sit alone in the dark
Everything, everything,
The drip of the bathroom tap,
The creak of the sofa spring,
The wind in the air-shaft, all
Making the same remark
Stupidly, stupidly,
Over and over again.

Father, what have I done?
Answer me, Father, how
Can I answer the tactless wall
Or the pompous furniture now?
Answer them . . .

GABRIEL

No, you must.

JOSEPH

How then am I to know,
Father, that you are just?
Give me one reason.

GABRIEL

No.

JOSEPH

All I ask is one
Important and elegant proof
That what my Love had done
Was really at your will
And that your will is Love.

GABRIEL

No, you must believe;
Be silent, and sit still.

II

NARRATOR

For the perpetual excuse
Of Adam for his fall—'My little Eve,
God bless her, did beguile me and I ate.'
    For his insistence on a nurse,

79

All service, breast, and lap, for giving Fate
Feminine gender to make girls believe
That they can save him, you must now atone,
 Joseph, in silence and alone;
While she who loves you makes you shake with fright,
Your love for her must tuck you up and kiss good night.

 For likening Love to war, for all
The pay-off lines of limericks in which
The weak resentful bar-fly shows his sting,
 For talking of their spiritual
Beauty to chorus-girls, for flattering
The features of old gorgons who are rich,
For the impudent grin and Irish charm
 That hides a cold will to do harm,
Today the roles are altered; you must be
The Weaker Sex whose passion is passivity.

 For those delicious memories
Cigars and sips of brandy can restore
To old dried boys, for gallantry that scrawls
 In idolatrous detail and size
A symbol of aggression on toilet walls,
For having reasoned—'Woman is naturally pure
Since she has no moustache,' for having said,
 'No woman has a business head,'
You must learn now that masculinity,
To Nature, is a non-essential luxury.

 Lest, finding it impossible
To judge its object now or throatily
Forgive it as eternal God forgives,
 Lust, tempted by this miracle
To more ingenious evil, should contrive
A heathen fetish from Virginity
To soothe the spiritual petulance

Of worn-out rakes and maiden aunts,
Forgetting nothing and believing all,
You must behave as if this were not strange at all.

Without a change in look or word,
You both must act exactly as before;
Joseph and Mary shall be man and wife
    Just as if nothing had occurred.
There is one World of Nature and one Life;
Sin fractures the Vision, not the Fact; for
The Exceptional is always usual
    And the Usual exceptional.
To choose what is difficult all one's days
As if it were easy, that is faith. Joseph, praise.

III

SEMI-CHORUS

Joseph, Mary, pray for those
Misled by moonlight and the rose,
For all in our perplexity.
Lovers who hear a distant bell
That tolls from somewhere in their head
Across the valley of their dream—
'All those who love excessively
Foot or thigh or arm or face
Pursue a louche and fatuous fire
And stumble into Hell'—
Yet what can such foreboding seem
But intellectual talk
So long as bodies walk
An earth where Time and Space
Turn Heaven to a finite bed
And Love into desire?
Pray for us, enchanted with

The green Bohemia of that myth
Where knowledge of the flesh can take
The guilt of being born away,
Simultaneous passions make
One eternal chastity:
Pray for us romantics, pray.

Joseph, Mary, pray for us,
Independent embryos who,
Unconscious in another, do
Evil as each creature does
In every definite decision
To improve; for even in
The germ-cell's primary division
Innocence is lost and sin,
Already given as a fact,
Once more issues as an act.

Joseph, Mary, pray for all
The proper and conventional
Of whom this world approves.
Pray for us whose married loves
Acquire so readily
The indolent fidelity
Of unaired beds, for us to whom
Domestic hatred can become
A habit-forming drug, whose will
To civil anarchy,
Uses disease to disobey
And makes our private bodies ill.
O pray for our salvation
Who take the prudent way,
Believing we shall be exempted

82

From the general condemnation
Because our self-respect is tempted
To incest not adultery:
O pray for us, the bourgeoisie.

BOY'S SEMI-CHORUS

Joseph, Mary, pray
For us children as in play
Upon the nursery floor
We gradually explore
Our members till our jealous lives
Have worked through to a clear
But trivial idea
Of that whence each derives
A vague but massive feel
Of being individual.
O pray for our redemption; for
Tho will that occupies
Our sensual infancy
Already is mature
And cold immediately
Beget upon our flesh far more
Expressions of its disbelief
Than we shall manage to conceive
In a long life of lies.

CHORUS

Blessed Woman,
Excellent Man,
Redeem for the dull the
Average Way,
That common ungifted
Natures may
Believe that their normal
Vision can
Walk to perfection.

83

THE SUMMONS

I

STAR OF THE NATIVITY

I am that star most dreaded by the wise,
For they are drawn against their will to me,
Yet read in my procession through the skies
The doom of orthodox suphrosyne:
I shall discard their major preservation,
All that they know so long as no one asks;
I shall deprive them of their minor tasks
In free and legal households of sensation,
Of money, picnics, beer, and sanitation.

Beware. All those who follow me are led
Onto that Glassy Mountain where are no
Footholds for logic, to that Bridge of Dread
Where knowledge but increases vertigo:
Those who pursue me take a twisting lane
To find themselves immediately alone
With savage water or unfeeling stone,
In labyrinths where they must entertain
Confusion, cripples, tigers, thunder, pain.

THE FIRST WISE MAN

To break down Her defences
    And profit from the vision
That plain men can predict through an
    Ascesis of their senses,
With rack and screw I put Nature through
    A thorough inquisition:
But She was so afraid that if I were disappointed
I should hurt Her more that Her answers were disjointed—

84

I did. I didn't. I will. I won't.
She is just as big a liar, in fact, as we are.
  To discover how to be truthful now
  Is the reason I follow this star.

THE SECOND WISE MAN

  My faith that in Time's constant
  Flow lay real assurance
Broke down on this analysis—
  At any given instant
All solids dissolve, no wheels revolve,
  And facts have no endurance—
And who knows if it is by design or pure inadvertence
That the Present destroys its inherited self-importance?
  With envy, terror, rage, regret,
We anticipate or remember but never are.
  To discover how to be living now
  Is the reason I follow this star.

THE THIRD WISE MAN

  Observing how myopic
  Is the Venus of the Soma,
The concept Ought would make, I thought,
  Our passions philanthropic,
And rectify in the sensual eye
  Both lens-flare and lens-coma:
But arriving at the Greatest Good by introspection
And counting the Greater Number, left no time for affec-
    tion,
  Laughter, kisses, squeezing, smiles:
And I learned why the learned are as despised as they are.
  To discover how to be loving now
  Is the reason I follow this star.

The weather has been awful,
  The countryside is dreary,
Marsh, jungle, rock; and echoes mock,
  Calling our hope unlawful;
But a silly song can help along
  Yours ever and sincerely:
At least we know for certain that we are three old sinners,
That this journey is much too long, that we want our
    dinners,
  And miss our wives, our books, our dogs,
But have only the vaguest idea why we are what we are.
  To discover how to be human now
  Is the reason we follow this star.

STAR OF THE NATIVITY

Descend into the fosse of Tribulation,
Take the cold hand of Terror for a guide;
Below you in its swirling desolation
Hear tortured Horror roaring for a bride:
O do not falter at the last request
But, as the huge deformed head rears to kill.
Answer its craving with a clear I Will;
Then wake, a child in the rose-garden, pressed
Happy and sobbing to your lover's breast.

II

NARRATOR

Now let the wife look up from her stove, the husband
Interrupt his work, the child put down its toy,
That His voice may be heard in our Just Society
  Who under the sunlight
Of His calm, possessing the good earth, do well. Pray
Silence for Caesar: stand motionless and hear

In a concourse of body and concord of soul
  His proclamation.

RECITATIVE

CITIZENS OF THE EMPIRE, GREETING. ALL MALE PERSONS
WHO SHALL HAVE ATTAINED THE AGE OF TWENTY-ONE
YEARS OR OVER MUST PROCEED IMMEDIATELY TO THE VIL-
LAGE, TOWNSHIP, CITY, PRECINCT OR OTHER LOCAL ADMIN-
ISTRATIVE AREA IN WHICH THEY WERE BORN AND THERE
REGISTER THEMSELVES AND THEIR DEPENDENTS IF ANY
WITH THE POLICE. WILFUL FAILURE TO COMPLY WITH THIS
ORDER IS PUNISHABLE BY CONFISCATION OF GOODS AND
LOSS OF CIVIL RIGHTS.

NARRATOR

You have been listening to the voice of Caesar
Who overcame implacable Necessity
By His endurance and by His skill has subdued the
  Welter of Fortune.
It is meet, therefore, that, before dispersing
In pious equanimity to obey His orders,
With well-tuned instruments and grateful voices
  We should praise Caesar.

III

FUGAL-CHORUS

Great is Caesar: He has conquered Seven Kingdoms.
The First was the Kingdom of Abstract Idea:
Last night it was Tom, Dick and Harry; tonight it is S's
    with P's;
Instead of inflexions and accents
There are prepositions and word-order;
Instead of aboriginal objects excluding each other
There are specimens reiterating a type;

Instead of wood-nymphs and river-demons,
There is one unconditioned ground of Being.
Great is Caesar: God must be with Him.

Great is Caesar: He has conquered Seven Kingdoms.
The Second was the Kingdom of Natural Cause:
Last night it was Sixes and Sevens; tonight it is One and
      Two;
Instead of saying, 'Strange are the whims of the Strong,'
We say, 'Harsh is the Law but it is certain';
Instead of building temples, we build laboratories;
Instead of offering sacrifices, we perform experiments;
Instead of reciting prayers, we note pointer-readings;
Our lives are no longer erratic but efficient.
Great is Caesar: God must be with Him.

Great is Caesar; He has conquered Seven Kingdoms.
The Third was the Kingdom of Infinite Number:
Last night it was Rule-of-Thumb, tonight it is To-a-T;
Instead of Quite-a-lot, there is Exactly-so-many;
Instead of Only-a-few, there is Just-these;
Instead of saying, 'You must wait until I have counted,'
We say, 'Here you are. You will find this answer correct';
Instead of a nodding acquaintance with a few integers
The Transcendentals are our personal friends.
Great is Caesar: God must be with Him.

Great is Caesar: He has conquered Seven Kingdoms.
The Fourth was the Kingdom of Credit Exchange:
Last night it was Tit-for-Tat, tonight it is C.O.D.;
When we have a surplus, we need not meet someone with a
      deficit;
When we have a deficit, we need not meet someone with a
      surplus;
Instead of heavy treasures, there are paper symbols of
      value;

88

Instead of Pay at Once, there is Pay when you can;
Instead of My Neighbour, there is Our Customers;
Instead of Country Fair, there is World Market.
Great is Caesar: God must be with Him.

Great is Caesar; He has conquered Seven Kingdoms.
The Fifth was the Kingdom of Inorganic Giants:
Last night it was Heave-Ho, tonight it is Whee-Spree;
When we want anything, They make it;
When we dislike anything, They change it;
When we want to go anywhere, They carry us;
When the Barbarian invades us, They raise immovable
        shields;
When we invade the Barbarian, They brandish irresistible
        swords;
Fate is no longer a fiat of Matter, but a freedom of Mind.
Great is Caesar: God must be with Him.

Great is Caesar: He has conquered Seven Kingdoms.
The Sixth was the Kingdom of Organic Dwarfs:
Last night it was Ouch-Ouch, tonight it is Yum-Yum;
When diseases waylay us, They strike them dead;
When worries intrude on us, They throw them out;
When pain accosts us, They save us from embarrassment;
When we feel like sheep, They make us lions;
When we feel like geldings, They make us stallions;
Spirit is no longer under Flesh, but on top
Great is Caesar: God must be with Him.

Great is Caesar: He has conquered Seven Kingdoms.
The Seventh was the Kingdom of Popular Soul:
Last night it was Order-Order, tonight it is Hear-Hear;
When he says, You are happy, we laugh;
When he says, You are wretched, we cry;
When he says, It is true, everyone believes it;
When he says, It is false, no one believes it;

When he says, This is good, this loved;
When he says, That is bad, that is hated.
Great is Caesar: God must be with Him.

IV

NARRATOR

These are stirring times for the editors of newspapers:
History is in the making; Mankind is on the march.
The longest aqueduct in the world is already
Under construction; the Committees on Fen-Drainage
And Soil-Conservation will issue very shortly
Their Joint Report; even the problems of Trade Cycles
And Spiralling Prices are regarded by the experts
As practically solved; and the recent restrictions
Upon aliens and free-thinking Jews are beginning
To have a salutary effect upon public morale.
True, the Western seas are still infested with pirates,
And the rising power of the Barbarian in the North
Is giving some cause for uneasiness; but we are fully
Alive to these dangers; we are rapidly arming; and both
Will be taken care of in due course: then, united
In a sense of common advantage and common right,
Our great Empire shall be secure for a thousand years.
    If we were never alone or always too busy,
Perhaps we might even believe what we know is not true:
But no one is taken in, at least not all of the time;
In our bath, or the subway, or the middle of the night,
We know very well we are not unlucky but evil,
That the dream of a Perfect State or No State at all,
To which we fly for refuge, is a part of our punishment.
    Let us therefore be contrite but without anxiety,
For Powers and Times are not gods but mortal gifts from
        God;
Let us acknowledge our defeats but without despair,

For all societies and epochs are transient details,
Transmitting an everlasting opportunity
That the Kingdom of Heaven may come, not in our Pre-
      sent
And not in our Future, but in the Fullness of Time.
Let us pray.

V

CHORALE

Our Father whose creative Will
    Asked Being for us all
Confirm it that Thy Primal Love
May weave in us the freedom of
The actually deficient on
    The justly actual.

Though written by Thy children with
    A smudged and crooked line
The Word is ever legible
Thy Meaning unequivocal
And for Thy Goodness even sin
    Is valid as a sign.

Inflict Thy promises with each
    Occasion of distress
That from our incoherence we
May learn to put our trust in Thee
And brutal fact persuade us to
    Adventure Art and Peace.

THE VISION OF THE SHEPHERDS

I

THE FIRST SHEPHERD

The winter night requires our constant attention
Watching that water and good-will
Warmth and well-being may still be there in the morning.

THE SECOND SHEPHERD

For behind the spontaneous joy of life
There is always a mechanism to keep going.

THE THIRD SHEPHERD

And someone like us is always there.

THE FIRST SHEPHERD

We observe that those who assure us their education
And money would do us such harm
How real we are just as we are and how they envy us
For it is the centreless tree
And the uncivilized robin who are the truly happy
Have done pretty well for themselves:

THE SECOND SHEPHERD

Nor can we help noticing how those who insist that
We ought to stand up for our rights
And how important we are keep insisting also
That it doesn't matter a bit
If one of us gets arrested or injured, for
It is only our numbers that count.

THE THIRD SHEPHERD
In a way they are right,

THE FIRST SHEPHERD
                    But to behave like a cogwheel
When one knows one is no such thing

THE SECOND SHEPHERD
Merely to add to a crowd with one's passionate body,
    Is not a virtue.

THE THIRD SHEPHERD
                What is real
About us all is that each of us is waiting.

THE FIRST SHEPHERD
    That is why we are able to bear
Ready-made clothes, second-hand art and opinions
    And being washed and ordered about;

THE SECOND SHEPHERD
That is why you should not take our conversation
    Too seriously, nor read too much
Into our songs;

THE THIRD SHEPHERD
            Their purpose is mainly to keep us
From watching the clock all the time.

THE FIRST SHEPHERD
For, though we cannot say why, we know that something
    Will happen:

THE SECOND SHEPHERD
            What we cannot say,

THE THIRD SHEPHERD

Except that it will not be a reporter's item
Of unusual human interest;

THE FIRST SHEPHERD

That always means something unpleasant.

THE SECOND SHEPHERD

But one day or
The next we shall hear the Good news.

II

THE THREE SHEPHERDS

Levers nudge the aching wrist;
'You are free
No to be,
Why exist?'
Wheels a thousand times a minute
Mutter, stutter,
'End the self you cannot mend,
Did you, friend, begin it?'
And the streets
Sniff at our defeats.
Then who is the Unknown
Who answers for our fear
As if it were His own
So that we reply
Till the day we die;
'No, I don't know why,
But I'm glad I'm here'?

III

Unto you a Child,
A Son is given.
Praising, proclaiming
The ingression of Love,
Earth's darkness invents
The blaze of Heaven,
And frigid silence
Meditates a song;
For great joy has filled
The narrow and the sad,
While the emphasis
Of the rough and big,
The abiding crag
And wandering wave,
Is on forgiveness:
Sing Glory to God
And good-will to men,
All, all, all of them.
Run to Bethlehem.

SHEPHERDS

Let us run to learn
How to love and run;
Let us run to Love.

CHORUS

Now all things living,
Domestic or wild,
With whom you must share
Light, water, and air,
And suffer and shake
In physical need,

95

The sullen limpet,
The exuberant weed,
The mischievous cat,
And the timid bird,
Are glad for your sake
As the new-born Word
Declares that the old
Authoritarian
Constraint is replaced
By His Covenant,
And a city based
On love and consent
Suggested to men,
All, all, all of them.
Run to Bethlehem.

SHEPHERDS

Let us run to learn
How to love and run;
Let us run to Love.

CHORUS

The primitive dead
Progress in your blood,
And generations
Of the unborn, all
Are leaping for joy
In your reins today
When the Many shall,
Once in your common
Certainty of this
Child's lovableness,
Resemble the One,
That after today
The children of men

May be certain that
The Father Abyss
Is affectionate
To all Its creatures,
All, all, all of them.
Run to Bethlehem.

AT THE MANGER

I

MARY

O shut your bright eyes that mine must endanger
With their watchfulness; protected by its shade
Escape from my care: what can you discover
From my tender look but how to be afraid?
Love can but confirm the more it would deny.
  Close your bright eye.

Sleep. What have you learned from the womb that bore
      you
But an anxiety your Father cannot feel?
Sleep. What will the flesh that I gave do for you,
Or my mother love, but tempt you from His will?
Why was I chosen to teach His Son to weep?
  Little One, sleep.

Dream. In human dreams earth ascends to Heaven
Where no one need pray nor ever feel alone.
In your first few hours of life here, O have you
Chosen already what death must be your own?
How soon will you start on the Sorrowful Way?
  Dream while you may.

II

FIRST WISE MAN

Led by the light of an unusual star,
We hunted high and low.

SECOND WISE MAN
                        Have travelled far,
For many days, a little group alone
With doubts, reproaches, boredom, the unknown.

THIRD WISE MAN
Through stifling gorges.

FIRST WISE MAN
                        Over level lakes,

SECOND WISE MAN
Tundras intense and irresponsive seas.

THIRD WISE MAN
In vacant crowds and humming silences,

FIRST WISE MAN
By ruined arches and past modern shops,

SECOND WISE MAN
Counting the miles,

THIRD WISE MAN
                        And the absurd mistakes.

THE THREE WISE MEN
O here and now our endless journey stops.

FIRST SHEPHERD
We never left the place where we were born,

SECOND SHEPHERD
Have only lived one day, but every day,

99

THIRD SHEPHERD

Have walked a thousand miles yet only worn
The grass between our work and home away.

FIRST SHEPHERD

Lonely we were though never left alone.

SECOND SHEPHERD

The solitude familiar to the poor
Is feeling that the family next door,
The way it talks, eats, dresses, loves, and hates,
Is indistinguishable from one's own.

THIRD SHEPHERD

Tonight for the first time the prison gates
Have opened.

FIRST SHEPHERD

          Music and sudden light

SECOND SHEPHERD

Have interrupted our routine tonight,

THIRD SHEPHERD

And swept the filth of habit from our hearts.

THE THREE SHEPHERDS

O here and now our endless journey starts.

WISE MEN

Our arrogant longing to attain the tomb,

SHEPHERDS

Our sullen wish to go back to the womb,

WISE MEN

To have no past,

SHEPHERDS

No future,

TUTTI

Is refused.

And yet, without our knowledge, Love is used
Our weakness as a guard and guide.

We bless

WISE MEN

Our lives' impatience,

SHEPHERDS

Our lives' laziness,

TUTTI

And bless each other's sin, exchanging here

WISE MEN

Exceptional conceit

SHEPHERDS

With average fear.

TUTTI

Released by Love from isolating wrong,
Let us for Love unite our various song,
Each with his gift according to his kind
Bringing this child his body and his mind.

III

WISE MEN

Child, at whose birth we would do obsequy
For our tall errors of imagination,
Redeem our talents with your little cry.

SHEPHERDS

Clinging like sheep to the earth for protection,
We have ventured far in any direction:
    Wean, Child, our aging flesh away
    From its childish way.

WISE MEN

Love is more serious than Philosophy
Who sees no humour in her observation
That Truth is knowing that we know we lie.

SHEPHERDS

When, to escape what our memories are thinking,
We go out at nights and stay up drinking,
    Stay then with our sick pride and mind
    The forgetful mind.

WISE MEN

Love does not will enraptured apathy;
Fate plays the passive role of dumb temptation
To wills where Love can doubt, affirm, deny.

SHEPHERDS

When, chafing at the rule of old offences,
We run away to the sea of the senses,
    On strange beds then O welcome home
    Our horror of home.

WISE MEN

Love knows of no somatic tyranny;
For homes are built for Love's accommodation
By bodies from the void they occupy.

SHEPHERDS

When, exhausting our wills with our evil courses,
We demand the good-will of cards and horses,
    Be then our lucky certainty
    Of uncertainty.

WISE MEN

Love does not fear substantial anarchy,
But vividly expresses obligation
With movement and in spontaneity.

SHEPHERDS

When, feeling the great boots of the rich on our
        faces,
We live in the hope of one day changing places,
    Be then the truth of our abuse
    That we abuse.

WISE MEN

The singular is not Love's enemy;
Love's possibilities of realisation
Require an Otherness that can say *I*

SHEPHERDS

When in dreams the beasts and cripples of resent-
        ment
Rampage and revel to our hearts' contentment,
    Be then the poetry of hate
    That replaces hate.

103

WISE MEN

Not In but With our time Love's energy
Exhibits Love's immediate operation;
The choice to love is open till we die.

SHEPHERDS

O Living Love, by your birth we are able
Not only, like the ox and ass of the stable,
  To love with our live wills, but love,
  Knowing we love.

TUTTI

O Living Love replacing phantasy,
O Joy of life revealed in Love's creation;
Our mood of longing turns to indication:
Space is the Whom our loves are needed by,
Time is our choice of How to love and Why

THE MEDITATION OF SIMEON

SIMEON

As long as the apple had not been entirely digested, as long as there remained the least understanding between Adam and the stars, rivers and horses with whom he had once known complete intimacy, as long as Eve could share in any way with the moods of the rose or the ambitions of the swallow, there was still a hope that the effects of the poison would wear off, that the exile from Paradise was only a bad dream, that the Fall had not occurred in fact.

CHORUS

When we woke, it was day; we went on weeping.

SIMEON

As long as there were any roads to amnesia and anaesthesia still to be explored, any rare wine or curiosity of cuisine as yet untested, any erotic variation as yet unimagined or unrealised, any method of torture as yet undevised, any style of conspicuous waste as yet unindulged, any eccentricity of mania or disease as yet unrepresented, there was still a hope that man has not been poisoned but transformed, that Paradise was not an eternal state from which he had been forever expelled, but a childish state which he had permanently outgrown, that the Fall had occurred by necessity.

CHORUS

We danced in the dark, but were not deceived.

SIMEON

As long as there were any experiments still to be undertaken in restoring that order in which desire had once rejoiced to be reflected, any code of equity and obligation upon which some society had not yet been founded, any species of property of which the value had not yet been appreciated, any talent that had not yet won private devotion and public honour, any rational concept of the Good or intuitive feeling for the Holy that had not yet found its precise and beautiful expression, any technique of contemplation or ritual of sacrifice and praise that had not yet been properly conducted, any faculty of mind or body that had not yet been thoroughly disciplined, there was still a hope that some antidote might be found, that the gates of Paradise had indeed slammed to, but with the exercise of a little patience and ingenuity would be unlocked, that the Fall had occurred by accident.

CHORUS

Lions came loping into the lighted city.

SIMEON

Before the Positive could manifest Itself specifically, it was necessary that nothing should be left that negation could remove; the emancipation of Time from Space had first to be complete, the Revolution of the Images, in which the memories rose up and cast into subjection the senses by whom hitherto they had been enslaved, successful beyond their wildest dreams, the mirror in which the Soul expected to admire herself so perfectly polished that her natural consolation of vagueness should be utterly withdrawn.

CHORUS

We looked at our Shadow, and, Lo, it was lame.

SIMEON

Before the Infinite could manifest Itself in the finite, it was necessary that man should first have reached that

106

point along his road to Knowledge where, just as it rises from the swamps of Confusion onto the sunny slopes of Objectivity, it forks in opposite directions towards the One and the Many; where, therefore, in order to proceed at all, he must decide which is Real and which only Appearance, yet at the same time cannot escape the knowledge that his choice is arbitrary and subjective.

CHORUS

Promising to meet, we parted forever.

SIMEON

Before the Unconditional could manifest Itself under the conditions of existence, it was necessary that man should first have reached the ultimate frontier of consciousness, the secular limit of memory beyond which there remained but one thing for him to know, his Original Sin, but of this it is impossible for him to become conscious because it is itself what conditions his will to knowledge. For as long as he was in Paradise he could not sin by any conscious intention or act: his as yet unfallen will could only rebel against the truth by taking flight into an unconscious lie; he could only eat of the Tree of the Knowledge of Good and Evil by forgetting that its existence was a fiction of the Evil One, that there is only the Tree of Life.

CHORUS

The bravest drew back on the brink of the Abyss.

SIMEON

From the beginning until now God spoke through His prophets. The Word aroused the uncomprehending depths of their flesh to a witnessing fury, and their witness was this: that the Word should be made Flesh. Yet their witness could only be received as long as it was vaguely misunderstood, as long as it seemed either to be neither impossible nor necessary, or necessary but not impossible, or impossible but not necessary; and the prophecy could not therefore be fulfilled. For it could only be fulfilled when it was no longer possible to receive, because it was clearly understood as absurd. The Word could not be made Flesh until men had reached a state of absolute contradiction between clarity and despair in which they would have no choice but either to accept absolutely or to reject absolutely, yet in their choice there should be no element of luck, for they would be fully conscious of what they were accepting or rejecting.

CHORUS

The eternal spaces were congested and depraved.

SIMEON

But here and now the Word which is implicit in the Beginning and in the End is become immediately explicit, and that which hitherto we could only passively fear as the incomprehensible I AM, henceforth we may actively love with comprehension that HE IS. Wherefore, having seen Him, not in some prophetic vision of what might be, but with the eyes of our own weakness as to what actually is, we are bold to say that we have seen our salvation.

CHORUS

Now and forever, we are not alone.

SIMEON

By the event of this birth the true significance of all other events is defined, for of every other occasion it can be said that it could have been different, but of this birth it is the case that it could in no way be other than it is. And by the existence of this Child, the proper value of all other existences is given, for of every other creature it can be said that it has extrinsic importance but of this Child it is the case that He is in no sense a symbol.

CHORUS

We have right to believe that we really exist.

SIMEON

By Him is dispelled the darkness wherein the fallen will cannot distinguish between temptation and sin, for in Him we become fully conscious of Necessity as our freedom to be tempted, and of Freedom as our necessity to have faith. And by Him is illuminated the time in which we execute those choices through which our freedom is realized or prevented, for the course of History is predictable in the degree to which all men love themselves, and spontaneous in the degree to which each man loves God and through Him his neighbour.

CHORUS

The distresses of choice are our chance to be blessed.

SIMEON

Because in Him the Flesh is united to the Word without magical transformation, Imagination is redeemed from promiscuous fornication with her own images. The tragic conflict of Virtue with Necessity is no longer confined to the Exceptional Hero; for disaster is not the impact of a curse upon a few great families, but issues continually from the hubris of every tainted will. Every invalid is Roland defending the narrow pass against hopeless odds, every stenographer Brunnhilde refusing to renounce her lover's ring which came into existence through the renunciation of love.

109

Nor is the Ridiculous a species any longer of the Ugly; for since of themselves all men are without merit, all are ironically assisted to their comic bewilderment by the Grace of God. Every Cabinet Minister is the woodcutter's simple-minded son to whom the fishes and the crows are always whispering the whereabouts of the Dancing Water or the Singing Branch, every heiress the washerwoman's butter-fingered daughter on whose pillow the fairy keeps laying the herb that could cure the Prince's mysterious illness.

Nor is there any situation which is essentially more or less interesting than another. Every tea-table is a battle-field littered with old catastrophes and haunted by the vague ghosts of vast issues, every martyrdom an occasion for flip cracks and sententious oratory.

Because in Him all passions find a logical In-Order-That, by Him is the perpetual recurrence of Art assured.

CHORUS

Safe in His silence, our songs are at play.

SIMEON

Because in Him the Word is united to the Flesh without loss of perfection, Reason is redeemed from incestuous fixation on her own Logic, for the One and the Many are simultaneously revealed as real. So that we may no longer, with the Barbarians, deny the Unity, asserting that there are as many gods as there are creatures, nor, with the philosophers, deny the Multiplicity, asserting that God is One who has no need of friends and is indifferent to a World of Time and Quantity and Horror which He did not create, nor, with Israel, may we limit the co-inherence of the One and the Many to a special case, asserting that God is only concerned with and of concern to that People whom out of all that He created He has chosen for His own.

For the Truth is indeed One, without which is no salvation, but the possibilities of real knowledge are as many as are the creatures in the very real and most exciting universe that God creates with and for His love, and it is not Nature which is one public illusion, but we who have each our many private illusions about Nature.

Because in Him abstraction finds a passionate For-The-Sake-Of, by Him is the continuous development of Science assured.

CHORUS

Our lost Appearances are saved by His love.

SIMEON

And because of His visitation, we may no longer desire God as if He were lacking: our redemption is no longer a question of pursuit but of surrender to Him who is always and everywhere present. Therefore at every moment we pray that, following Him, we may depart from our anxiety into His peace.

CHORUS

Its errors forgiven, may our Vision come home.

THE MASSACRE OF
THE INNOCENTS

I

HEROD

Because I am bewildered, because I must decide, because my decision must be in conformity with Nature and Necessity, let me honour those through whom my nature is by necessity what it is.

> To Fortune—that I have become Tetrarch, that I have escaped assassination, that at sixty my head is clear and my digestion sound.
>
> To my Father—for the means to gratify my love of travel and study.
>
> To my Mother—for a straight nose.
>
> To Eva, my coloured nurse—for regular habits.
>
> To my brother, Sandy, who married a trapeze-artist and died of drink—for so refuting the position of the Hedonists.
>
> To Mr. Stewart, nicknamed The Carp, who instructed me in the elements of geometry through which I came to perceive the errors of the tragic poets.
>
> To Professor Lighthouse—for his lectures on The Peloponnesian War.
>
> To the stranger on the boat to Sicily—for recommending to me Brown on Resolution.
>
> To my secretary, Miss Button—for admitting that my speeches were inaudible.

There is no visible disorder. No crime—what could be more innocent than the birth of an artisan's child? Today has been one of those perfect winter days, cold, brilliant, and utterly still, when the bark of a shepherd's dog carries for miles, and the great wild mountains come up quite close to the city walls, and the mind feels intensely awake, and this evening as I stand at this window high up in the citadel there is nothing in the whole magnificent panorama of plain and mountains to indicate that the Empire is threatened by a danger more dreadful than any invasion of Tartars on racing camels or conspiracy of the Praetorian Guard.

Barges are unloading soil fertilizer at the river wharves. Soft drinks and sandwiches may be had in the inns at reasonable prices. Allotment gardening has become popular. The highway to the coast goes straight up over the mountains and the truck-drivers no longer carry guns. Things are beginning to take shape. It is a long time since anyone stole the park benches or murdered the swans. There are children in this province who have never seen a louse, shopkeepers who have never handled a counterfeit coin, women of forty who have never hidden in a ditch except for fun. Yes, in twenty years I have managed to do a little. Not enough, of course. There are villages only a few miles from here where they still believe in witches. There isn't a single town where a good bookshop would pay. One could count on the fingers of one hand the people capable of solving the problem of Achilles and the Tortoise. Still it is a beginning. In twenty years the darkness has been pushed back a few inches. And what, after all, is the whole Empire, with its few thousand square miles on which it is possible to lead the Rational Life, but a tiny patch of light compared with those immense areas of barbaric night that surround it on all sides, that incoherent wilderness of rage and terror, where Mongolian idiots are regarded as sacred and mothers who give birth to twins are instantly put to death, where malaria is treated by yelling, where warriors of superb courage obey the commands of hysterical female impersonators, where the best cuts of meat are reserved for the dead, where, if a white blackbird has been seen, no more work may be done that day, where it is firmly believed that the world was created by a giant with three heads or that the notions of the stars are controlled from the liver of a rogue elephant?

Yet even inside this little civilized patch itself, where, at the cost of heaven knows how much grief and bloodshed, it has been made unnecessary for anyone over the age of twelve to believe in fairies or that First Causes reside in mortal and finite objects, so many are still homesick for that disorder wherein every passion formerly enjoyed a frantic licence. Caesar flies to his hunting lodge pursued by ennui; in the faubourgs of the Capital, Society grows savage, corrupted by silks and scents, softened by sugar and hot water, made insolent by theatres and attractive slaves; and everywhere, including this province, new prophets spring up every day to sound the old barbaric note.

I have tried everything. I have prohibited the sale of crystals and ouija-boards; I have slapped a heavy tax on playing cards; the courts are empowered to sentence alchemists to hard labour in the mines; it is a statutory offence to turn tables or feel bumps. But nothing is really effective. How can I expect the masses to be sensible when, for instance, to my certain knowledge, the captain of my own guard wears an amulet against the Evil Eye, and the richest merchant in the city consults a medium over every important transaction?

Legislation is helpless against the wild prayer of longing that rises, day in, day out, from all these households under my protection: 'O God, put away justice and truth for we cannot understand them and do not want them. Eternity would bore us dreadfully. Leave Thy heavens and come down to our earth of waterclocks and hedges. Become our uncle. Look after Baby, amuse Grandfather, escort Madam to the Opera, help Willy with his home-work, introduce Muriel to a handsome naval officer. Be interesting and weak like us, and we will love you as we love ourselves.'

114

Reason is helpless, and now even the Poetic Compromise no longer works, all those lovely fairy tales in which Zeus, disguising himself as a swan or a bull or a shower of rain or what-have-you, lay with some beautiful woman and begot a hero. For the Public are grown too sophisticated. Under all the charming metaphors and symbols, it detects the stern command, 'Be and act heroically'; behind the myth of divine origin, it senses the real human excellence that is a reproach to its own baseness. So, with a bellow of rage, it kicks Poetry downstairs and sends for Prophecy. 'Your sister has just insulted me. I asked for a God who should be as like me as possible. What use to me is a God whose divinity consists in doing difficult things that I cannot do or saying clever things that I cannot understand? The God I want and intend to get must be someone I can recognize immediately without having to wait and see what he says or does. There must be nothing in the least extraordinary about him. Produce him at once, please, I'm sick of waiting.'

Today, apparently, judging by the trio who came to see me this morning with an ecstatic grin on their scholarly faces, the job has been done. 'God has been born,' they cried, 'we have seen him ourselves. The World is saved. Nothing else matters.'

One needn't be much of a psychologist to realize that if this rumour is not stamped out now, in a few years it is capable of diseasing the whole Empire, and one doesn't have to be a prophet to predict the consequences if it should.

Reason will be replaced by Revelation. Instead of Rational Law, objective truths perceptible to any who will undergo the necessary intellectual discipline, and the same for all, Knowledge will degenerate into a riot of subjective visions—feelings in the solar plexus induced by under-nourishment, angelic images generated by fevers or drugs, dream warnings inspired by the sound of falling water.

Whole cosmogonies will be created out of some forgotten personal resentment, complete epics written in private languages, the daubs of school children ranked above the greatest masterpieces.

Idealism will be replaced by Materialism. Priapus will only have to move to a good address and call himself Eros to become the darling of middle-aged women. Life after death will be an eternal dinner party where all the guests are twenty years old. Diverted from its normal and wholesome outlet in patriotism and civic or family pride, the need of the materialistic Masses for some visible Idol to worship will be driven into totally unsocial channels where no education can reach it. Divine honours will be paid to silver teapots, shallow depressions in the earth, names on maps, domestic pets, ruined windmills, even in extreme cases, which will become increasingly common, to headaches, or malignant tumours, or four o'clock in the afternoon.

Justice will be replaced by Pity as the cardinal human virtue, and all fear of retribution will vanish. Every cornerboy will congratulate himself: 'I'm such a sinner that God had to come down in person to save me. I must be a devil of a fellow.' Every crook will argue: 'I like committing crimes. God likes forgiving them. Really the world is admirably arranged.' And the ambition of every young cop will be to secure a deathbed repentance. The New Aristocracy will consist exclusively of hermits, bums, and permanent invalids. The Rough Diamond, the Consumptive Whore, the bandit who is good to his mother, the epileptic girl who has a way with animals will be the heroes and heroines of the New Tragedy when the general, the statesman, and the philosopher have become the butt of every farce and satire.

Naturally this cannot be allowed to happen. Civilization must be saved even if this means sending for the military, as I suppose it does. How dreary. Why is it that in the end

116

civilization always has to call in these professional tidiers to whom it is all one whether it be Pythagoras or a homicidal lunatic that they are instructed to exterminate. O dear, Why couldn't this wretched infant be born somewhere else? Why can't people be sensible? I don't want to be horrid. Why can't they see that the notion of a finite God is absurd? Because it is. And suppose, just for the sake of argument, that it isn't, that this story is true, that this child is in some inexplicable manner both God and Man, that he grows up, lives, and dies, without committing a single sin? Would that make life any better? On the contrary it would make it far, far worse. For it could only mean this; that once having shown them how, God would expect every man, whatever his fortune, to lead a sinless life in the flesh and on earth. Then indeed would the human race be plunged into madness and despair. And for me personally at this moment it would mean that God had given me that power to destroy Himself. I refuse to be taken in. He could not play such a horrible practical joke. Why should He dislike me so? I've worked like a slave. Ask anyone you like. I read all official dispatches without skipping. I've taken elocution lessons. I've hardly ever taken bribes. How dare He allow me to decide? I've tried to be good. I brush my teeth every night. I haven't had sex for a month. I object. I'm a liberal. I want everyone to be happy. I wish I had never been born.

II

SOLDIERS

When the Sex War ended with the slaughter of the Grand-
    mothers,
They found a bachelor's baby suffocating under them;
Somebody called him George and that was the end of it:
    They hitched him up to the Army.

George, you old débutante,
How did you get in the Army?

In the Retreat from Reason he deserted on his rocking-
    horse
And lived on a fairy's kindness till he tired of kicking her;
He smashed her spectacles and stole her cheque-book and
    mackintosh
  Then cruised his way back to the Army.
  George, you old numero,
  How did you get in the Army?

Before the Diet of Sugar he was using razor-blades
And exited soon after with an allergy to maidenheads;
He discovered a cure of his own, but no one would patent it,
  So he showed up again in the Army.
  George, you old flybynight,
  How did you get in the Army?

When the Vice Crusades were over he was hired by some
    Muscovites
Prospecting for deodorants among the Eskimos;
He was caught by a common cold and condemned to the
    whiskey mines,
  But schemozzled back to the Army.
  George, you old Emperor,
  How did you get in the Army?

Since Peace was signed with Honour he's been minding his
    business;
But, whoops, here comes His idleness, buttoning his uni-
    form;
Just in tidy time to massacre the Innocents;
  He's come home to roost in the Army.
  George, you old matador,
  Welcome back to the Army.

118

III

On the Left are grinning dogs, peering down into a solitude
    too deep to fill with roses.
On the Right are sensible sheep, gazing up at a pride where
    no dream can grow.
Somewhere in these unending wastes of delirium is a lost
    child, speaking of Long Ago in the language of
    wounds.
Tomorrow, perhaps, he will come to himself in Heaven.
But here Grief turns her silence, neither in this direction,
    nor in that, nor for any reason.
And her coldness now is on the earth forever.

THE FLIGHT INTO EGYPT

I

JOSEPH

Mirror, let us through the glass
No authority can pass.

MARY

Echo, if the strong should come,
Tell a white lie or be dumb.

VOICES OF THE DESERT

It was visitors' day at the vinegar works
In Tenderloin Town when I tore my time;
A sorrowful snapshot was my sinful wage:
Was that why you left me, elusive bones?
  Come to our bracing desert
  Where eternity is eventful,
    For the weather-glass
    Is set at Alas,
  The thermometer at Resentful.

MARY

The Kingdom of the Robbers lies
Between Time and our memories;

JOSEPH

Fugitives from Space must cross
The waste of the Anonymous.

VOICES OF THE DESERT

How should he figure my fear of the dark?
The moment he can he'll remember me,

The silly, he looked in the cellar for fun,
And his dear little doggie shall die in his arms.
Come to our old-world desert
Where everyone goes to pieces;
You can pick up tears
For souvenirs
Or genuine diseases.

JOSEPH

Geysers and volcanoes give
Sudden comical relief;

MARY

And the vulture is a boon
On a dull hot afternoon.

VOICES OF THE DESERT

All Father's nightingales knew their place,
The gardens were loyal; look at them now.
The roads are so careless, the rivers so rude,
My studs have been stolen; I must speak to the sea.
Come to our well-run desert
Where anguish arrives by cable,
And the deadly sins
May be bought in tins
With instructions on the label.

MARY

Skulls recurring every mile
Direct the thirsty to the Nile;

JOSEPH

And the jackal's eye at night
Forces Error to keep right.

121

In a land of lilies I lost my wits,
Nude as a number all night I ran
With a ghost for a guest along green canals;
By the waters of waking I wept for the weeds.
 Come to our jolly desert
 Where even the dolls go whoring;
  Where cigarette-ends
  Become intimate friends,
 And it's always three in the morning.

JOSEPH AND MARY

Safe in Egypt we shall sigh
For lost insecurity;
Only when her terrors come
Does our flesh feel quite at home.

II

RECITATIVE

Fly, Holy Family, from our immediate rage,
That our future may be freed from our past; retrace
 The footsteps of law-giving
 Moses, back through the sterile waste,
Down to the rotten kingdom of Egypt, the damp
Tired delta where in her season of glory our
 Forefathers sighed in bondage;
 Abscond with the Child to the place

That their children dare not revisit, to the time
They do not care to remember; hide from our pride
 In our humiliation;
 Fly from our death with our new life.

III

Well, so that is that. Now we must dismantle the tree,
Putting the decorations back into their cardboard boxes—
Some have got broken—and carrying them up to the attic.
The holly and the mistletoe must be taken down and burnt,
And the children got ready for school. There are enough
Left-overs to do, warmed-up, for the rest of the week—
Not that we have much appetite, having drunk such a lot,
Stayed up so late, attempted—quite unsuccessfully—
To love all of our relatives, and in general
Grossly overestimated our powers. Once again
As in previous years we have seen the actual Vision and
       failed
To do more than entertain it as an agreeable
Possibility, once again we have sent Him away,
Begging though to remain His disobedient servant,
The promising child who cannot keep His word for long.
The Christmas Feast is already a fading memory,
And already the mind begins to be vaguely aware
Of an unpleasant whiff of apprehension at the thought
Of Lent and Good Friday which cannot, after all, now
Be very far off. But, for the time being, here we all are,
Back in the moderate Aristotelian city
Of darning and the Eight-Fifteen, where Euclid's geometry
And Newton's mechanics would account for our experience,
And the kitchen table exists because I scrub it.
It seems to have shrunk during the holidays. The streets
Are much narrower than we remembered; we had forgotten
The office was as depressing as this. To those who have seen
The Child, however dimly, however incredulously,
The Time Being is, in a sense, the most trying time of all
For the innocent children who whispered so excitedly
Outside the locked door where they knew the presents to be
Grew up when it opened. Now, recollecting that moment

We can repress the joy, but the guilt remains conscious;
Remembering the stable where for once in our lives
Everything became a You and nothing was an It.
And craving the sensation but ignoring the cause,
We look round for something, no matter what, to inhibit
Our self-reflection, and the obvious thing for that purpose
Would be some great suffering. So, once we have met the Son,
We are tempted ever after to pray to the Father;
'Lead us into temptation and evil for our sake.'

They will come, all right, don't worry; probably in a form
That we do not expect, and certainly with a force
More dreadful than we can imagine. In the meantime
There are bills to be paid, machines to keep in repair,
Irregular verbs to learn, the Time Being to redeem
From insignificance. The happy morning is over,
The night of agony still to come; the time is noon:
When the Spirit must practise his scales of rejoicing
God will cheat no one, not even the world of its triumph.

IV

CHORUS

He is the Way.
Follow Him through the Land of Unlikeness;
You will see rare beasts, and have unique adventures.

He is the Truth.
Seek Him in the Kingdom of Anxiety;
You will come to a great city that has expected your return
    for years.

He is the Life.
Love Him in the World of the Flesh;
And at your marriage all its occasions shall dance for joy.